DATE D

STEPHEN
CRANE

EDITED AND WITH AN
INTRODUCTION BY HAROLD BLOOM

BLOOM'S MAJOR DRAMATISTS

Aeschylus

Anton Chekhov

Aristophanes

Berthold Brecht

Euripides

Henrik Ibsen

Ben Johnson

Christopher Marlowe

Arthur Miller

Eugene O'Neill

Shakespeare's Comedies

Shakespeare's Histories

Shakespeare's Romances

Shakespeare's Tragedies

George Bernard Shaw

Neil Simon

Sophocles

Oscar Wilde

Tennessee Williams

August Wilson

BLOOM'S MAJOR NOVELISTS

Jane Austen

The Brontës

Willa Cather

Stephen Crane

Charles Dickens

Fyodor Dostoevsky

William Faulkner

F. Scott Fitzgerald

Thomas Hardy

Nathaniel Hawthorne

Ernest Hemingway

Henry James

James Joyce

D. H. Lawrence

Toni Morrison

John Steinbeck

Stendhal

Leo Tolstoy

Mark Twain

Alice Walker

Edith Wharton

Virginia Woolf

BLOOM'S MAJOR WORLD POETS

Geoffrey Chaucer

Emily Dickinson

John Donne

T. S. Eliot

Robert Frost

Langston Hughes

John Milton

Edgar Allan Poe

Poets of World War I

Shakespeare's Poems & Sonnets

Alfred, Lord Tennyson

Walt Whitman

William Wordsworth

BLOOM'S MAJOR SHORT STORY WRITERS

William Faulkner

F. Scott Fitzgerald

Ernest Hemingway

O. Henry

James Joyce

Herman Melville

Flannery O'Connor

Edgar Allan Poe

J. D. Salinger

John Steinbeck

Mark Twain

Eudora Welty

STEPHEN
CRANE

COMPREHENSIVE RESEARCH
AND STUDY GUIDE

BLOOM'S
MAJOR
NOVELISTS

EDITED AND WITH AN INTRODUCTION
BY HAROLD BLOOM

© 2002 by Chelsea House Publishers, a subsidiary of
Haights Cross Communications.

Introduction © 2002 by Harold Bloom.

Printed and bound in the United States of America.

First Printing
1 3 5 7 9 8 6 4 2

Library of Congress Cataloging-in-Publication Data
applied for

ISBN 0-7910-6345-3

Chelsea House Publishers
1974 Sproul Road, Suite 400
Broomall, PA 19008-0914

The Chelsea House World Wide Web address is
http://www.chelseahouse.com

Series Editor: Matt Uhler

Contributing Editor: Janyce Marson

Produced by Publisher's Services, Santa Barbara, California

Contents

User's Guide   7

Editor's Note   8

Introduction   10

Biography of Stephen Crane   13

Plot Summary of *Maggie: A Girl of the Streets*   19

List of Characters in *Maggie: A Girl of the Streets*   25

Critical Views on *Maggie: A Girl of the Streets*

  Rosalie Murphy Baum on the Burden of Myth   27

  Aida Farrag Graff on Metaphor and Metonymy   29

  Lawrence E. Hussman Jr. on the Fate of the Fallen Woman   31

  Sydney J. Krause on Naturalism   32

  George T. Novotny on Classical Influences   34

  Alice Hall Petry on Crane's Familiarity with the Art World   36

  Karen E. Waldron on the Journalistic Style   38

Plot Summary of *The Red Badge of Courage*   41

List of Characters in *The Red Badge of Courage*   51

Critical Views on *The Red Badge of Courage*

  Jean R. Halladay on Carlylean Echoes   52

  Harold Kaplan on the Civil War as Religious Revelation   54

  Thomas L. Kent on Epistemological Uncertainty   56

  John J. McDermott on Symbolism and Psychological Realism   57

  James Nagel on Literary Impression   59

  Donald Pease on History and Heroic Attributes   61

  Donald Pizer on the Ambiguity of Henry Fleming's Character   63

  Kirk M. Reynolds on James Nagel's Reading of Henry Fleming   65

  Ben Satterfield on the Novel as Humanistic Work of Art   67

  Daniel Shanahan on the Nature of Martial Virtue   69

  Michael Schneider on Mythic Elements of Quest-Romance   71

  Robert Shulman on Trauma in Crane's Myth of the Civil War   73

  Henry Binder on the *Red Badge of Courage* Nobody Knows   75

  Carol B. Hafer on Irony in *The Red Badge of Courage*   77

  Jean Cazemajou on the "Religion of Peace" and the War Archetype   78

  N. E. Dunn on the Common Msan's *Iliad*   80

  Bill Brown on the War Game   82

James M. Cox on the Purity of War   84
Harold Beaver on the Hero as Victim   86
Alfred Habegger on Crane's Representation of Speech   88

Works by Stephen Crane   90
Works About Stephen Crane   91
Index of Themes and Ideas   95

User's Guide

This volume is designed to present biographical, critical, and bibliographical information on the author's best-known or most important works. Following Harold Bloom's editor's note and introduction is a detailed biography of the author, discussing major life events and important literary accomplishments. A plot summary of each novel follows, tracing significant themes, patterns, and motifs in the work.

A selection of critical extracts, derived from previously published material from leading critics, analyzes aspects of each work. The extracts consist of statements from the author, if available, early reviews of the work, and later evaluations up to the present. A bibliography of the author's writings (including a complete list of all works written, cowritten, edited, and translated), a list of additional books and articles on the author and his or her work, and an index of themes and ideas in the author's writings conclude the volume.

～

Harold Bloom is Sterling Professor of the Humanities at Yale University and Henry W. and Albert A. Berg Professor of English at the New York University Graduate School. He is the author of over 20 books, including *Shelley's Mythmaking* (1959), *The Visionary Company* (1961), *Blake's Apocalypse* (1963), *Yeats* (1970), *A Map of Misreading* (1975), *Kabbalah and Criticism* (1975), *Agon: Toward a Theory of Revisionism* (1982), *The American Religion* (1992), *The Western Canon* (1994), and *Omens of Millennium: The Gnosis of Angels, Dreams, and Resurrection* (1996). *The Anxiety of Influence* (1973) sets forth Professor Bloom's provocative theory of the literary relationships between the great writers and their predecessors. His most recent books include *Shakespeare: The Invention of the Human*, a 1998 National Book Award finalist, and *How to Read and Why*, which was published in 2000.

Professor Bloom earned his Ph.D. from Yale University in 1955 and has served on the Yale faculty since then. He is a 1985 MacArthur Foundation Award recipient, served as the Charles Eliot Norton Professor of Poetry at Harvard University in 1987–88, and has received honorary degrees from the universities of Rome and Bologna. In 1999, Professor Bloom received the prestigious American Academy of Arts and Letters Gold Medal for Criticism.

Currently, Harold Bloom is the editor of numerous Chelsea House volumes of literary criticism, including the series BLOOM'S NOTES, BLOOM'S MAJOR DRAMATISTS, BLOOM'S MAJOR NOVELISTS, MAJOR LITERARY CHARACTERS, MODERN CRITICAL VIEWS, MODERN CRITICAL INTERPRETATIONS, and WOMEN WRITERS OF ENGLISH AND THEIR WORKS.

Editor's Note

My Introduction centers upon the nihilistic element in the epic impressionism of *The Red Badge of Courage*.

Critical views on *Maggie: A Girl of the Streets* commence with Rosalie Murphy Baum whose emphasis is the influence upon Maggie of her parents' aggressive alcoholism. For Aida Farrag Graff, Maggie and Jimmie are also marred by their world of strife, while Lawrence E. Hussman Jr. compares Maggie to Dreiser's Sister Carrie.

Sidney J. Krause finds a split in Crane's naturalism, at once surrealistic and obvious, after which George T. Novotny finds traces of Pope's Homer in *Maggie*. The realism of William Hogarth is seen as one of Crane's sources by Alice Hall Petry, while Karen E. Waldron finds journalistic representation to be Maggie's mode.

The Red Badge of Courage is aptly related to Carlyle's *Sartor Resartus* by Jean R. Halladay, after which Harold Kaplan analyzes religious imagery in Crane's battle epic.

Thomas L. Kent finds an unsettling of the reader's stance toward the story to be a crucial strand in *Red Badge*, while John J. Mcdermott traces Crane's fusion of symbolism and realism. For James Nagel, Henry Fleming is an Impressionist lens through whom the reader must peer, after which Donald Pease shows Crane's freedom from historical or moral perspectivism.

The ambiguity of Henry Fleming is stressed by Donald Pizer, while Kirk M. Reynolds disputes James Nagel's reading. Ben Satterfield regards *Red Badge* as essentially affirmative, after which Daniel Shanahan emphasizes the initial passivity of Fleming.

Michael Schneider reads *Red Badge* as quest-romance, while Robert Shulman finds trauma to be the defining mark of Crane's myth of the Civil War. The deletions that truncated the novel are studied by Henry Binder, after which Carol B. Hafer considers some of *Red Badge*'s ironies.

Jean Cazemajou balances the war narrative of Crane's book with its interspersed visions of peace, while N. E. Dunn argues for *Red Badge* as the American version of Homeric epic. For Bill Brown, the ironic vision of the American male as athlete haunts the book, after which James M. Cox brilliantly summarizes *Red Badge*'s achievement.

Harold Beaver powerfully invokes Dante in defining Stephen Crane's personal dilemmas, while Alfred Habegger commends the vernacularly mastery of *Red Badge*'s prose.

Introduction

HAROLD BLOOM

Rereading *The Red Badge of Courage,* it is difficult to believe that it was written by a young man not yet twenty-four, who had never seen battle. Dead of tuberculosis at twenty-eight, Stephen Crane nevertheless had written a canonical novel, three remarkable stories, and a handful of permanent poems. He was a singular phenomenon: his father, grandfather and great-uncle all were evangelical Methodists, intensely puritanical. Crane, precocious both as man-of-letters and as journalist, kept living out what Freud called "fantasies of rescue," frequently with prostitutes. His common-law marriage, which sustained him until his early death, was with Cora Taylor, whom he first met when she was madame of a Florida bordello. Incongruously, Crane—who was *persona non-grata* to the New York City police—lived a brief, exalted final phase in England, where he became close to the great novelists Joseph Conrad and Henry James, both of whom greatly admired Crane's writing.

Had Crane lived, he doubtless would have continued his epic impressions of war, and confirmed his status as a crucial forerunner of Ernest Hemingway. And yet his actual observations of battle, of Americans against Spaniards in Cuba, and of Greeks against Turks, led to war-writing greatly inferior to his imaginings in *The Red Badge of Courage.* Perhaps Crane would have developed in other directions, had he survived. It is difficult to envision Crane improving upon *The Red Badge of Courage,* which is better battle-writing than Hemingway and Norman Mailer could accomplish. The great visionaries of warfare—Homer, Virgil, Shakespeare, Tolstoy—necessarily are beyond Crane's art, but in American literature he is surpassed in this mode only by the Cormac McCarthy of *Blood Meridian.* McCarthy writes in the baroque, high rhetorical manner of Melville and Faulkner. Crane, a very original impressionist, was a Conradian before he read Conrad. I sometimes hear Kipling's prose style in Crane, but the echoes are indistinct and fleeting, almost as though the battlefield visionary had just read *The Jungle Book.* Kipling, though also a great journalist, could not provide Crane with a paradigm to assist in the recreation of the bloody battle of Chancellorsville (May 2–4, 1863). Harold Beaver suggests that Stendhal and Tolstoy did that labor for Crane, which is highly feasible, and Beaver is also interesting in suggesting that Crane invented a kind of expressionism in his hallucinatory, camera-eye visions, as here in Chapter 7 of the *Red Badge*:

> Once he found himself almost into a swamp. He was obliged to walk upon bog tufts and watch his feet to keep from the oily mire. Pausing at one time to look about him he saw, out at some black water, a small animal pounce in and emerge directly with a gleaming fish.
>
> The youth went again into the deep thickets. The brushed branches made a noise that drowned the sound of cannon. He walked on, going from obscurity into promises of a greater obscurity.
>
> At length he reached a place where the high, arching boughs made a chapel. He softly pushed the green doors aside and entered. Pine needles were a gentle brown carpet. There was a religious half light.
>
> Near the threshold he stopped, horror-stricken at the sight of a thing.
>
> He was being looked at by a dead man who was seated with his back against a columnlike tree. The corpse was dressed in a uniform that once had been blue, but was now faded to a melancholy shade of green. The eyes, staring at the youth, had changed to the dull hue to be seen on the side of a dead fish. The mouth was open. Its red had changed to an appalling yellow. Over the gray skin of the face ran little ants. One was trundling some sort of a bundle along the upper lip.

This is a kind of pure, visual irony, nihilistic and parodistic, beyond meaning, or with meanings beyond control. On a grander scale, here is the famous account of the color sergeant's death in Chapter 19:

> Over the field went the scurrying mass. It was a handful of men splattered into the faces of the enemy. Toward it instantly sprang the yellow tongues. A vast quantity of blue smoke hung before them. A mighty banging made ears valueless.
>
> The youth ran like a madman to reach the woods before a bullet could discover him. He ducked his head low, like a football player. In his haste his eyes almost closed, and the scene was a wild blur. Pulsating saliva stood at the corners of his mouth.

Within him, as he hurled himself forward, was born a love, a despairing fondness for this flag which was near him. It was a creation of beauty and invulnerability. It was a goddess, radiant, that bended its form with an imperious gesture to him. It was a woman, red and white, hating and loving, that called him with the voice of his hopes. Because no harm could come to it he endowed it with power. He kept near, as if it could be a saver of lives, and an imploring cry went from his mind.

In the mad scramble he was aware that the color sergeant flinched suddenly, as if struck by a bludgeon. He faltered, and then became motionless, save for his quivery knees.

He made a spring and a clutch at the pole. At the same instant his friend grabbed it from the other side. They jerked at it, stout and furious, but the color sergeant was dead, and the corpse would not relinquish its trust. For a moment there was a grim encounter. The dead man, swinging with bended back, seemed to be obstinately tugging, in ludicrous and awful ways, for the possession of the flag.

It was past in an instant of time. They wrenched the flag furiously from the dead man, and, as they turned again, the corpse swayed forward with bowed head. One arm swung high, and the curved hand fell with heavy protest on the friend's unheeding shoulder.

The flag and the color sergeant's corpse become assimilated to one another, and the phantasmagoria of the flag-as-woman is highly ambivalent, being both an object of desire, and potentially destructive: "hating and loving." Crane's vision again is nihilistic, and reminds us that even his title is an irony, since the ultimate red badge of courage would be a death-wound. ❀

Biography of
Stephen Crane

At two o'clock in the morning on September 16, 1896, while walking along Sixth Avenue with two chorus girls, Stephen Crane witnessed a policeman arrest these young women in the trumped up charge that they were attempting to solicit two men. One of these women, Dora Clark, was locked up that same night—calling out to Crane that she wanted to appear before the magistrate. While she may not have been soliciting at the time of her arrest, the sergeant in charge was willing to uphold her arrest because he knew her to be a common prostitute. Crane decided to become her advocate and challenge the New York City Police Department. The following morning, Crane waited inside the Jefferson Market Courthouse until he could address the judge and proclaim Dora's innocence. A reporter from the *New York Journal* observed what transpired, not realizing that Crane was a well-known writer. He documented his observations and, on September 17, the Stephen Crane story had made headlines all over New York—the *New York Journal* proclaimed, "He Wore No Red Badge of Courage, But Pluckily Saved a Girl from the Law." By the next day, September 18, the favorable publicity bestowed on Crane took on a decidedly negative tone with such newspapers as the *Chicago Dispatch* stated that his "association with women in scarlet is not necessarily a 'Red Badge of Courage.'"

Coincidentally, it was also at this time that Crane's publisher, S. S. McClure, introduced him to the New York City Police Commissioner, Theodore Roosevelt (who would later become President of the United States only a few years after Stephen's death). McClure was considering having Crane write a story about the New York police. Roosevelt, having been a strong advocate of police reform ever since his campaign in 1895, had felt "demoralized by the . . . venality and blackmail" within the department. When Roosevelt first made Crane's acquaintance, he was a great admirer of his work, especially *The Red Badge of Courage,* and owned all of Crane's books. Both he and Crane shared a love of books, especially of Tolstoy and stories of the West and the hard-riding cowboys. In August of that year, Crane sent Roosevelt an autographed copy of *George's Mother.* Nevertheless, whatever positive feelings Roosevelt may have had for Crane and his work, he soon made an abrupt change following

Crane's impolitic response to an unfortunate public event. During that same August, William Jennings Bryan was in the midst of campaigning as the Democratic candidate for the presidency at Madison Square Garden when a spectacular security fiasco took place. Gatecrashers arrived in force leaving legitimate ticket holders unable to attend the event. The affair received a lot of bad publicity from the press. Although Roosevelt wrote to Crane in an attempt to excuse the police on grounds of inexperience with this type of mob, it is unclear whether Crane ever received his letter. Crane wrote a scathing article in the August 20 edition of the *Gazette,* referring to the police department's mismanagement as a "shameful performance" while lauding the former and very corrupt police chief, Thomas F. Byrnes. Crane's criticism did not end there. In his August 27 column, Crane again attacked Roosevelt—this time for his rigid enforcement of the blue laws which he believed lead to the police department's persecution of the city's harmless traders. In response to his vitriol, the New York City police set to work trying to gather incriminating evidence about Crane's character. Their efforts included a raid on his apartment as well as attempts at proving his consorting with chorus girls and prostitutes. Roosevelt, a man of impossibly high moral standards, would come to view Stephen Crane as objectionable for displaying a distressing lack of inhibition.

It was also during the summer of 1896 that Crane lived with Amy Leslie, the well-known drama critic of the *Chicago Daily News,* at 121 West 27th Street. Though she was Crane's senior by 16 years, she was considered to be a very beautiful woman. Her photographs always depicted her as being elaborately dressed with a beautiful smile. Leslie lead a glamorous life attending theater openings and parties, and she was considered to be brilliant and witty, at times demonstrating a very sharp tongue. Having started out as an actress and singer herself, Leslie was known to be nurturing towards actors and generous in her reviews. At the time she met Crane, she may still have been married to the comedian Harry Brown. After their summer together Leslie returned to her apartment in Chicago—the couple continued to see each other when they could. Only Crane's side of the correspondence between the two lovers still exists and, from those letters, it is apparent that Leslie was in some kind of trouble. Believing that she would return to New York to live with Crane after his return from Cuba, she entrusted him with eight hundred dollars, which he was to deposit in a bank in New York. Crane, taking the easier course, apparently put her money in his own account. Leslie was enraged at his casual handling of her money. Leslie's letters soon indicated that she knew Crane had taken a new lover—accusations Crane would flatly deny though he knew their romance was over.

Later in that year, while on his way to cover Cuba's insurrection against Spanish rule in Cuba, Crane stopped in Jacksonville, Florida, which at that time had become the country's major filibustering port. American sympathies towards the Cuban insurgents was high, having been inflamed by the yellow journalism of Hearst's *New York Journal* and Joseph Pulitzer's *New York World*. Along with the strong sympathy, there was also the potential to make money by smuggling arms to the insurgents. Stephen Crane was of the belief that the idea of smuggling arms was a romantic appeal for clandestine activities, referring to it as a "delicious bit of outlawry in the evening of the nineteenth century." Upon his arrival in Jacksonville, Crane registered at the best hotel under the alias Samuel Carleton. While visiting the smoky back rooms of seedy waterfront saloons and local brothels he met Cora Taylor, six years his senior, and the proprietress of her aptly named Hotel de Dream. At 31, Taylor prided herself on looking young. Like his former sweetheart, Amy Leslie, Cora was short, blond, attractive and her manner of dressing suggested an affluent way of life. Interestingly, Taylor came from a fine and very literate family in Boston. Her paternal great grandfather had been a prominent Boston art dealer, her father was a painter and, thus, she had been raised in an atmosphere of artistic appreciation. Following her parents death, which left her a wealthy young woman, Cora soon departed from the mores of her social background. At not yet twenty years of age, Cora lived out of wedlock with a man while working as a hostess at a gambling house, the London Club, followed by two brief and unsuccessful marriages. A well-known personality in Jacksonville, an intriguing woman who had a mixture of scandal and propriety about her, Cora ran her "sporting house" as an elegant establishment. She even had a man called Professor to play the piano for her "guests." Stephen Crane would meet her at a dinner party shortly after his arrival in Jacksonville, and it was at this time he revealed Samuel Carleton's true identity. Cora was delighted to make Crane's acquaintance as she had been reading one of his books and because he was a writer very much in vogue at that time. He would live with Cora for the last three years of his life. Crane's preference for a woman like Cora, is characteristic of his own rebellious personality and, further, of the lives of the socially-marginalized urban poor whom he observed and subsequently wrote about.

Indeed, Stephen Crane was forever resistant to his parents' strict religious beliefs and traditional notions of social propriety. Born on November 1, 1871 in Newark, New Jersey, Stephen was the son of a Methodist preacher, the Reverend Johnathan Townley Crane, who had once described mankind's condition as "one of inexpressible evil," destined to a hell of "eternal darkness and despair." Awarded a doctorate of divinity from Dickinson College in 1856, Reverend Crane wrote numerous articles and books declaiming the evils of dancing, novel reading, and intoxication. Though he was against slavery, he wanted to avoid a civil war and, thus, proposed a system of serfdom, similar to that of Russia. Stephen, on the other hand, though of a gentle temperament, would later become obsessed by war and violence culminating in the writing of his greatest novel, *The Red Badge of Courage.* His mother, Mary Helen Peck Crane was a kindly and devout woman who, although reconciled to the life of a minister's wife, including a series of frequent moves, nevertheless loved to paint and believed that she should be doing a lot more than household chores. As the mother of fourteen children, Stephen being the last, her responsibilities were endless.

Because his health was fragile as a child, there is a discrepancy among biographers as to when he started school. The authors of *The Crane Log* maintain that he began school in January, 1880 at the Mountain House School in Port Jervis, New York after an abbreviated start at the Main Street School. When his father died in February, 1880, Mrs. Crane and her younger children were required to leave the parsonage and eventually took up residence in Asbury Park, New Jersey some three years later. Asbury Park, a proud prohibition town, proved to be a haven for American Methodists in that it provided a safe refuge from life's temptations. It is here, in 1883, that Stephen enrolls in the sixth grade at the Asbury Park School, and where he writes his first known story, "Uncle Jake and the Bell Handle," a tale of two country bumpkins on a day's outing in the big city. On September 14, 1885, Stephen enrolls at his father's old school, Pennington Seminary, a rigid, coeducational boarding school just north of Trenton, an institution primarily intended to prepare young men for the seminary.

By the time Crane enrolled at Syracuse University in January 1891, he had already decided on a literary career. After moving into a spacious second-floor apartment with his roommate, Clarence N. Goodwin, Crane joined several clubs, among them the Nut-Brown Maiden, a coasting club; an eating group called the Tooth Pick Club, and Delta Upsilon's cricket club where he served as captain. Though he was of slight build, he immediately tried out for the baseball team, a game which he enjoyed playing since childhood, and for which he was already a legendary catcher. The Syracuse team was considered middling, but Crane was considered the best player of nine and one of the best catchers in Syracuse's history. Crane's scholastic achievements, however, were far from remarkable. He was a student of his own invention, registering for only one course, English literature, in the College of Liberal Arts. He preferred to relax in his room, reading newspapers, history books and literary masterpieces, among them *Faust, Anna Karenina,* and *War and Peace.* On June 12, 1891, Crane left Syracuse, declaring college to be "a waste of time." It was around this time that he began his career in journalism and began to immerse himself in the kind of lifestyle of which he was asked to write.

On the morning of August 17, 1892, Crane attended a lecture on the novelist William Dean Howells, delivered by Hamlin Garland, a young teacher from Boston and rising literary star. Crane listened with rapt attention to Garland's theory of realism in art and literature, which essentially held the view that true art must reflect contemporary American life in all its variety. In the following years, a great friendship evolved, with Garland and Crane discussing their two great passions—literature and baseball. In October of that year, Crane began making frequent trips to New York City, exploring the tenements, the Bowery, the saloons and dance halls, the brothels and flophouses. It was the world of the marginalized and dispossessed. It was also during this time that his mother died at the age of sixty-four. Crane had just turned twenty and, in the months following his mother's death, he wrote his Sullivan County Tales about four hapless men, innocents and social misfits, who wander through a mountainous forest, disconnected from the outside world. It is in these sketches that Crane makes full use of color as metaphor and dream imagery to express the unconscious mind. However, after a few jobs with New York newspapers, Crane lived a life of privation, moving into various seedy apartments with his artist friends. As a result of his own experience with poverty, and having received an assignment from the newly-formed Bacheller-Johnson Newspaper Syndicate to write about the Bowery, in 1893 Crane was asked to live amongst and write "An Experiment in Misery," a story about the sordid life of a flophouse, replete with "strange and unspeakable odors." It was an assignment which Crane relished and an experiment in living which he had no trouble adapting to. Shortly thereafter, Crane wrote, and published at his own expense, *Maggie: A Girl of the Streets.* However, although both Hamlin Garland and W. D. Howells admired the novel, it did not sell, and it is generally agreed among critics that the audience of the 1890s was looking for escapist fiction which would provide a distraction from the social and moral issues of the day. Crane's next literary endeavor would be his masterpiece, *The Red Badge of Courage,* where he would use the Civil War as his subject. As a story about the education and growth into manhood of the young Henry Fleming, it is a narrative which builds on several major literary traditions ranging from Homer to Shakespeare, and Herman Melville among others. It is a story in which personal identity is complex and ambiguous and, in this capacity, it is very modern. Crane's fortunes began to improve immediately when *Red Badge* was first published as a syndicated newspaper story in December, 1894. That same newspaper hired Stephen in 1895 to be a reporter in the American West and Mexico, an experience which lead to his writing "The Bridge Comes to Yellow Sky" and "The Blue Hotel." When *The Red Badge* appeared in book form in the fall of 1895, Crane received international acclaim at the age of 24.

On December 29, 1899, following a ball at which such literary greats as Henry James, H. G. Wells, George Gissing, and Joseph Conrad were guests, Stephen Crane suffered a lung hemorrhage which he tried to conceal from Cora. Crane continued to work from bed and in early February, 1900, was busy writing chapter after chapter of a new swashbuckling novel about an Irish blade named the O'Ruddy. Stephen Crane died on June 5, 1900. That same day, he had dictated more of his romance, now entitled *The O'Ruddy,* a narrative filled with the action of men galloping on horses through a Sussex rain. As Cora wrote in her notebook, Stephen was glad that she had cut his hair "during illness so that he would not be a bald old man." ❀

Plot Summary of
Maggie: A Girl of the Streets

The story begins with a street battle between rival gangs in the impoverished Bowery, with the "honor of Rum Alley" pitted against the Devil's Row contingent which is lead by Jimmie Johnson, and whose very names highlight the evils which accompany the poverty to which they are condemned. The scene is at once interminably violent and blindly savage. "On their small, convulsed faces there shone the grins of true assassins." When Jimmie finally ends up at the bottom of a pile of attackers, it is the angry and arrogant Pete, "with an air of challenge over his eye," who comes to his rescue. "Between his teeth, a cigar stump was tilted at the angle of defiance." But his "rescue" notwithstanding, Jimmie is soon embroiled in yet another fight, because in the larger context of this novel, it is simply not possible to be rescued from the devastating effects of urban poverty in such places as New York's Lower East Side.

Shortly after the break up of the second fight by Jimmie's father, we are then introduced to the terrible conditions of life in a Lower East Side tenement, "a dark region where, from a careening building, a dozen gruesome doorways gave up loads of babies to the street and gutter." But the return home is not to a safe haven, for we now witness the incessantly combative Jimmie get into a fight with his sister Maggie. Shortly thereafter, we encounter their alcoholic mother Mary who immediately flies into a rage. "The mother's massive shoulders heaved with anger. . . . She dragged him to an unholy sink, and, soaking a rag in water, began to scrub his lacerated face with it." This act is followed by her banishing the father from their flat. Not surprisingly, the father likewise seeks to escape the "living hell" by getting drunk, "determined upon a vengeful drunk" while the terrified children passively retreat from this brutal exchange. Indeed, Crane is also making a strong statement that slum life offers no hope of escape and, further, that this environment is devoid of any spiritual relief. "The little boy ran to the halls, shrieking like a monk in an earthquake." Though the frightened Jimmie is offered some temporary sanctuary by an elderly neighbor, "a gnarled and leathery personage who could don, at will, an expression of great virtue," there is scant reason to have any faith or credence from such a person. "Once, when a lady had dropped her purse on the sidewalk, the gnarled woman grabbed it and smuggled it with great dexterity beneath her cloak." To compound both our distrust and lack of confidence in her ability to shelter a child, she sends Jimmie on a dangerous mission to buy her some beer from a saloon where, not surprisingly, he is soon assailed by his own father who wants nothing more than to steal the beer from his young son. "The father wrenched the pail from the urchin. . . . There was a tremendous gulping movement and the beer was gone." When Jimmie finally returns home, both parents are drunk, exchanging "howls and curses, groans and shrieks, confusingly in chorus as if a battle were raging." Indeed, life in the slums is an unending tragedy, and the use of the word chorus here could even be seen as analogous to the chorus in a Greek tragedy which had the function of both participating in and commenting on the events taking place. Further, Crane is also implying that the reality of the slums resembles a life in a jungle in that the abject fright in which the children are forced to live makes them akin to animals who must hide in fear of those who seek to devour them. In her mother's presence, Maggie is seen eating "like a small pursued tigress," and both she and her brother are huddled in fright, "crouched until the ghost-mists of dawn appeared at the window."

After the passage of some considerable, but unspecified, time of several years, we learn that both the unremarkable father and the baby, Tommie, have died for some vague reasons and their presence quickly and sadly evaporates from both the world of the tenement and the consciousness of the reader. "The babe, Tommie died. He went away in a white, insignificant coffin." All this while Jimmie continues to grow up into a brooding young man, "sullen with thoughts of a hopeless altitude where grew fruit," that the sum total of his life experiences had presaged, a downtrodden human being who was gainsaid whatever happiness belonged to other more fortunate men. It is during these formative years in which he "menaced mankind at the intersection of streets" that Jimmie's character devolves into that of an increasingly bitter and hardened individual, who learned to "breathe maledictory defiance at the police." Chapter 4 provides a glimpse of the consequences of that devolving personality as Jimmie takes a job as a teamster driving horses through lower Manhattan. "In revenge, he resolved never to move out of the way of anything, until formidable circumstances . . . forced him to it." Indeed, this job makes Jimmie even more belligerent and alienated, so much so that he shuns all religion and faith. Devoid of all hope of a better way of life, Jimmie is spiritually lost, "for he himself could perceive that Providence had caused it clearly to be written."

Parallel to Jimmie's growing into manhood, Maggie manages to nurture and retain a certain beauty despite the ravages of the Bowery and the filth of Rum Alley. "She grew to be a most rare and wonderful production of a tenement district." When she does go to work in a sweatshop in the business of "turning out collars, the name of whose brand could be noted for its irrelevancy to anything in connection with collars," Crane emphasizes the extent to which the working poor are met with the same loss of identity they have known since childhood. But the most tragic consequence of poverty is Maggie's vulnerability to the advances of the boastful Pete, with whom she becomes infatuated. "There was valor and contempt for circumstances in the glance of his eye. He waved his hands like a man of the world, who dismisses religion and philosophy." And Maggie is equally susceptible to the same gullible adoration when Pete regales her with his tall tales of strength and manliness on the job, telling would-be troublemakers to "get deh hell outa here," and, most audaciously, of appreciation and commendation from his boss. "But deh boss . . . he says, 'Pete, yes done jes' right!'" But the sweet and innocent Maggie has no way of discerning Pete's dishonesty and false bravado and, sadly, falls prey to his vain promise of false hope in that she is still able to imagine the possibility of escaping the poverty and degradation into which she has been born. "Maggie perceived that here was the beau ideal of a man. . . . Under the trees of her dream-gardens there had always walked a lover."

No sooner does she begin to date Pete that he introduces her to the seedy world of leisure that accompanies their impoverished existence. She attends burlesque dances, where girls dance, "making profuse gesticulations" while "[a]n occasion man bent forward, intent upon the pink stockings" as well attending conventional melodramas where after "a carefully prepared crisis" the singer burst into the national anthem. Furthermore, the fantastical melodramas to which he takes her only serve to increase and perpetuate the unattainable lifestyle which she can only dream of. "Maggie always departed with raised spirits from the showing places of the melodrama. She rejoiced at the way in which the poor and virtuous eventually surmounted the wealthy and wicked." Her dates with Pete and the forms of entertainment to which he introduces her are tantamount to a very cruel joke. Though she does not realize it yet, she is doomed to live the life she was born to. To further emphasize this fact, one night Pete comes to call on Maggie, only to observe her drunken mother and belligerent brother embroiled in a violent argument. At this point, Mary launches into a vituperative denunciation against her daughter Maggie, telling her to "[g]o the hell an' good riddance." Thus, the prerequisite conditions are set for Maggie to go off with Pete, which in turn will lead to her seduction and final downfall.

On the following evening, Jimmie listens to their neighbor, the old woman, recount what she observed after Mary consigned Maggie to the devil. The old woman saw Maggie crying and heard her ask Pete if he loved her. "'It was deh funnies' t'ing I ever saw,' she cried, coming close to him and leering" and it also underscores a fundamental lack of understanding and respect for Maggie's plight by those who are made to suffer the same daily degradation and deprivation. Needless to say, Mary Johnson has no ability to see the harms she does when she heaps blame on her sweet and unsuspecting daughter nor, for that matter, her failure as a parent. "'Yeh've gone the deh devil, Mag Johnson. . . . Yer a disgrace the yer people.'" And it is only a short time afterwards that Jimmie and his friend Billie visit Pete at the bar in which he works with the purpose of a violent confrontation. After some preliminary provocative statements, a fight ensues, resulting in Pete and Billie getting arrested. It is important to note that although Jimmie abandons his friend Billie and manages to escape arrest, there is an underlying truth from which he can never flee—namely that he is forever condemned to the Bowery and the brutal life of poverty. Nor has he any ability to understand how that impoverished existence has molded his character.

A short time later, we now find Pete and Maggie at a very disreputable bar, "a hall of irregular shape," with Maggie now completely and tragically dependent on the disreputable Pete. Much to her detriment, Maggie still sees Pete as her savior, with "wealth and prosperity in his clothes," and the all but realized promise of a better way of life. "She thought of her former Rum Alley environment and turned to regard Pete's strong protecting fists. . . . She imagined a future rose-tinted. . . ." Needless to say, Maggie does not consider herself degraded or in any way diminished by Pete. "She would be disturbed by no apprehensions, so long as Pete adored her as he now said he did." Her irresponsible mother, on the other hand, wastes no time in casting blame and aspersion on her. "May Gawd curse her forever. . . . May she eat nothin' but stones and deh dirt in deh street," while Jimmie, who spends a fleeting moment wondering whether "all sisters, excepting his own, could advisedly be ruined," and, just as easily, he forgets this thought. It should be noted that Maggie's mother is equally adept at manipulating situations to her own advantage and does not hesitate to blame her uncontrollable, drunken rages on her daughter when confronted by the police.

Meanwhile, it has been three weeks since Maggie began living with Pete, during which "her spaniel-like dependence had been magnified." Pete, however, is about to show his true nature as he is easily seduced by a former acquaintance, Nellie, "a woman of brilliance and audacity," a woman who possesses a character similar to his. Though she herself is on a date, Nellie persuades Pete to leave with her with the result that he abandons Maggie along with Nellie's date. Maggie eventually begins to make her way back to her family's tenement.

During this time there is another portentous scene in which we are introduced to another, similarly forsaken woman wandering the streets alone at night. This woman turns out to be Hattie, a woman whom Jimmie had likewise rejected. "The forlorn woman had a peculiar face. . . . as if some one had sketched with cruel forefinger indelible lines about her mouth." And Hattie's chance encounter with Jimmie on this particular evening ends with her errant lover summarily dismissing her once again. But the reader soon returns to Maggie's and the events that unfold upon her return home. There she is treated like a pariah by both her mother and her brother as well as the neighborhood gossips. "Through the open doors curious eyes stared in at Maggie. . . . Women, without, bended toward each other and whispered, nodding their heads with airs of profound philosophy." Maggie has no choice but to leave as an exile, shunned by all except the old woman who offers her a place stay.

When the scene next reverts back to Pete at his bar the next day, he is disposing of the relationship with Maggie without further ado. "He saw no necessity for anyone's losing their equilibrium merely because their sister or their daughter had stayed away from home." When Maggie tries to talk to him, he angrily and summarily dismisses her, telling her to "go teh hell." Her fate is now inevitable and, thus, it is hardly surprising that she would fall into a life of prostitution, "a girl of the painted cohorts of the city." Shortly thereafter, on a rainy evening, amidst "the gloomy districts near the river, where the tall black factories shut in the street" a huge fat man in greasy clothes begins to follow her, we are left to guess at the outcome of this encounter as we lose sight of their destination. Meanwhile, the reader returns to a very drunk Pete who is sitting at a saloon, cavorting with several giggling women, who "nod their heads approvingly" at him. One of those silly women is Nellie. Pete eventually collapses, but first gives Nellie money while making an empty declaration of his love for her to which Nellie's responds that he is "a damn fool."

In the final scene, Jimmie delivers the news in a vague and deadpan announcement that "Mag's dead." In contrast to this tragic event, and tragically brief statement of fact, Mary Johnson launches into a highly melodramatic and wholly unconvincing act of uncontrollable grief and mourning, making a spectacle of herself. "The neighbors began to gather in the hall, staring in at the weeping woman as if watching the contortions of a dying dog." And her feigned forgiveness of her daughter, her "disobed'ent chil," is equally as empty. In a brief story in which the survivors are utterly and absolutely unable to extricate themselves from the world of the Lower East Side to which fate has condemned them, an early death becomes the only means of escape from a world where "[t]he varied sounds of life, made joyous by distance and seeming unapproachableness, came faintly and died away to silence." ❀

List of Characters in
Maggie: A Girl of the Streets

Maggie, the title character. Maggie Johnson is a young woman who grows up in the squalor and poverty of the Bowery in New York City's Lower East Side. While her mother, Mary, is an abusive alcoholic and her brother, Jimmie, is a brute, Maggie manages to grow up a beautiful young woman with the hope and desire for a better way of life. Maggie's downfall, however, occurs as the result of her love for Pete, a young man who appears to be confident and sophisticated, but who nevertheless abandons her. As a result of that abandonment, Maggie becomes a prostitute in order to earn a living, which further causes her to become the object of scandalous talk in the neighborhood. In the end, Maggie succumbs to her terrible environment and lifestyle, but the reason she dies is very unclear—she may have been a murder victim or, possibly, taken her own life. Nevertheless, Crane's message is very clear. Maggie is the victim of the impoverished economic and social conditions of the world she was born into and, most poignantly, was not able to escape.

Jimmie, Maggie's brother and Mary's son. Jimmie, the first character we hear about, is in the midst of a street battle. He is violent and devoid of compassion for the other children. He also lacks the ability to understand his own combative behavior. Having seduced and abandoned women he is guilty of the same abusive treatment as Maggie's seducer, Pete. Nevertheless, Jimmie hates Pete for what he has done to Maggie, while never recognizing that he has behaved the same way. Ironically, instead of having sympathy for Maggie, Jimmie blames his sister for causing the scandal. Though he has acquired the brutish characteristics necessary of the urban poverty which has molded his personality, Jimmie's survival is simply that and nothing more.

Mary, Maggie and Jimmie's mother. She is an abusive and vicious alcoholic, who is given over to uncontrollable outrage, spending much of her time destroying her physical environment. Her rage is so terrifying that Maggie runs away. Indeed, she is even the butt of joke within her own rough neighborhood. But Mary Johnson also has the audacity to criticize Maggie's behavior as immoral and, finally, she is also extremely manipulative as evidenced by her staging a scene of mourning for the daughter whom she never loved.

Pete, a friend of Jimmie Johnson and a very affected bartender. As a result of his talk about money and his pretense to offer a better way of life, he succeeds in seducing the innocent Maggie Johnson. However, he soon loses interest in Mary when his attention is turned to an equally pretentious and manipulative woman named Nellie. As it turns out, Nellie has no love for Peter, but was merely using him for his money.

Tommie, Maggie's youngest brother, dies early in the novel, a victim of his pernicious environment.

Father, of Maggie, Jimmie and Tommie, and husband of Mary. He is an alcoholic and casually abusive towards his children. He even resorts to stealing beer from Jimmie. The father dies early in the novel and Crane only gives him a last name

The old woman, has no name. She inhabits the same tenement house as the Johnson family and befriends the Johnson children. She even offers Maggie shelter after the young woman has been shunned by her own abusive mother.

Miss Smith, has only a brief appearance in the last scene of the novel. She encourages Mary Johnson into her false sentimental act of mourning for her deceased daughter Maggie.

Billie, a violent little Rum Alley child who first appears at the beginning of the narrative where he is embroiled in a street fight with Jimmie. Billie grows up into the same violent behavior as Jimmie and also becomes Jimmie's ally in his hatred towards Pete. ❀

Critical Views on
Maggie: A Girl of the Streets

ROSALIE MURPHY BAUM ON THE BURDEN OF MYTH

[Rosalie Murphy Baum is the author of "Work, Contentment and Identity in Aging Women in Literature" (1999) and "The Burden of Myth: The Role of the Farmer in American Literature" (1985). In the excerpt below from her article, "Alcoholism and Family Abuse in *Maggie* and *The Bluest Eye*," Baum discusses the role of alcoholism as a mode of expression of the competing needs for the individual characters to escape stress while bolstering their self-esteem.]

In 1893, Stephen Crane's *Maggie: A Girl of the Streets* depicted a young white girl and her two brothers growing up in the Bowery, with a father and mother who engage in vicious physical fights. Seventy-seven years later, in 1970, Toni Morrison's *The Bluest Eye* dramatized the plight of a black girl and her brother growing up in Lorain, Ohio, in an atmosphere of conjugal strife. In both works alcoholism plays an important role in the lives of the parents and thus of the children. But in both cases alcoholism is shown to be much more *caused* than causing. ⟨. . .⟩

On the societal and sub cultural levels, as well as on the individual, small-group and situational levels, drinking behavior is influenced by cultural factors. On the societal level, for example, drinking in the United States occurs in a society which recognizes and accepts drinking for many purposes. American society is one of many in which, in Edwin M. Lemert's words, drinking is "a culture pattern, a symptom of psychic stress, a symbolic protest, or a form of collective behavior." As a form of escapism (characteristic, according to Don Cahalen, Ira H. Cisin and Helen M. Crossley, of one-third of the men who drink and one-fourth of the women), it can be both a symptom of stress and "a symbolic protest"; as a means of compensating for loss of power—within the social structure or personal relationship—it can also be a symptom of stress and "a symbolic protest."

In addition, drunken aggressiveness is a cultural defense mechanism which serves to alleviate stress and hostility in America, and it is a defense mechanism that largely frees the aggressive drinker from guilt. The reasoning is that since alcohol releases inhibitions, the drinker may commit acts normally unacceptable to self-esteem or reputation without feeling directly responsible for these acts—as long as he can attribute their cause to alcohol. Alcohol serves as an "excuse" which is used by both the drinker and other family members in order to maintain an image of normalcy and nondeviancy to both themselves and their society. Thus, an accepted social custom—drinking—and an accepted, acknowledged result—aggression—allow the drinker to have the "time out" which Craig MacAndrew and Robert Edgerton identify as a learned behavior in which "the drunkard finds himself, if not beyond good and evil, at least partially removed from the accountability nexus in which he normally operates." ⟨. . .⟩

On the individual, small-group and situational levels, drinking behavior is also influenced by cultural factors. The fact that aggressive behavior frequently occurs in the presence of people of lower status can of course contribute to an understanding of the large number of spouse-abuse situations which involve a high degree of alcohol abuse: forty to ninety-five percent of the cases studied by Roger Langley and Richard C. Levy, eighty-three percent by Gisela Spieker. Spieker explains that an attack on a family member while intoxicated provides a feeling of "self-worth . . . frequently perceived as having 'power'"; it provides "the grounds for refusing to accept responsibility for one's own violent behavior"; and it occurs in a situation where one's behavior has "the least chance for negative consequences," a "safe zone." One usually is not going to lose a job or even have the police called in if one reserves one's aggression for family members. Further, Murray A. Straus suggests that cultural norms which support "a male-dominant balance of power in the family" and hence sexual inequality, which accept a high level of conflict and violence within the family structure and between siblings, and which legitimize physical punishment of the children within the family all establish the family as a base for "unintended training in violence." ⟨. . .⟩

—Rosalie Murphy Baum, "Alcoholism and Family Abuse in *Maggie* and *The Bluest Eye*," *Mosaic* 19, no. 3 (Summer 1986): pp. 91–93.

[Aida Farrag Graff is the author of "Metaphor and Metonymy: The Two Worlds of Crane's *Maggie*." In the excerpt below from her article, Graff discusses two rhetorical modes of perceiving and experiencing the external world.]

Stephen Crane describes *Maggie: A Girl of the Streets* in the following terms: "It tries to show that environment is a tremendous thing in the world and frequently shapes lives regardless. If one proves that theory one makes room in Heaven for all sorts of souls, notably an occasional street girl, who are not confidently expected to be there by many excellent people." Crane's reference to "Heaven" may suggest that he had in mind the moral aspect of environment rather than its purely material dimension; that he was thinking of environment in terms of the values that it projected. Nevertheless, his characters do move and interact in specific places that define and affect them. For as Elizabeth Bowen so aptly put it: "Nothing can happen nowhere." That is why I would like to examine in the following pages the aesthetic function of setting in *Maggie* through Roman Jakobson's metaphor/metonymy concept. ⟨. . .⟩

Maggie: A Girl of the Streets is the story of Maggie Johnson, her brother Jimmie, her seducer Pete, and ultimately the Johnson home. After an introductory chapter, of the remaining eighteen chapters, seven are devoted to depicting the Johnson home. Jimmie's emergence into adulthood and his fight with Pete occupy two chapters. Eight chapters are devoted to Maggie, while Pete holds the scene without her or Jimmie for one chapter. What becomes clear if one looks at these chapters as separate groupings, is that each character has his own definite space. Thus the tenement building defines the Johnson space, music halls and showplaces set off Maggie, while street corners define Jimmie. Pete's space is the fake splendour of the bar in which he works, as well as the smoky confines of a saloon booth in which we see him drunk at the end of the book. This kind of schematization is of limited use since characters share each other's spaces. However, it is in relation to a particular character that each of the settings has a function in the book. Furthermore, there are also different linguistic spaces in the book with its two different stylistic registers. Thus the inarticulate language of the characters strongly contrasts with the sophisticated language of the narrative voice. These two spaces, in turn, relate to the juxtaposition we have in the book between two distinct environments—the tenement and the city.

The opening pages of *Maggie* plunge the reader into a world of strife: "A little boy stood upon a heap of gravel for the honor of Rum Alley. He was throwing stones at howling urchins from Devil's Row, who were circling madly about the heap and pelting him." In his essay on the naturalist novel, Jacques Dubois notes that very often "la description inaugurale se fait protocole de lecture. Elle anticipe sur tout le roman." In the opening paragraph of this book, the group of children from Devil's Row behave in what will appear to be the Bowery norm. The image of the circle as they press upon Jimmie is repeated several times in the chapter: "cursing circle," "bobbing circle," "circle of little boys." As a microcosm of the world in which they live, their encirclement of Jimmie anticipates the whole sense of entrapment that defines Bowery life. For Maggie's subsequent tragedy occurs not only because of her warped perception of reality, but also because she is unable to break with her environment. Jimmie, on the other hand, has all the aggressiveness that will allow him to survive in it.

Having focussed the reader's attention upon the "circle" of fighting children, the narrative voice now diverts it towards some onlookers positioned at different points. The movement in this paragraph from watcher to watcher gradually removes the reader from the circle of fighting children. These onlookers are obviously close enough to watch what is going on, but each is a little further removed and evinces less active concern for the fight. Observing and watching become important motifs in the book as action is constantly perceived by an audience. One critic sees the whole structure of the novel in terms of a "play within a play" which "reinforces the idea that life must be viewed realistically, even if painfully." While the theatricality of Bowery life is an important structural element in the novel, what it really emphasizes is the lack of private spaces in that environment because the characters all subscribe to "a value system oriented toward approval by others, toward an audience." ⟨. . .⟩

—Aida Farrag Graff, "Metaphor and Metonymy: The Two Worlds of Crane's *Maggie*," *English Studies in Canada* 8, no. 4 (December 1982): pp. 422–424.

LAWRENCE E. HUSSMAN JR. ON THE FATE OF THE FALLEN WOMAN

[Lawrence E. Hussman Jr. is the author of "A Measure of Sister Carrie's Growth" (1980) and "Thomas Edison and Sister Carrie: A Source for Character and Theme" (1975). In the excerpt below from his article, "The Fate of the Fallen Woman in *Maggie* and *Sister Carrie*," Hussman discusses the "realistic veneer" which Crane applies to his novella.]

The two most famous turn-of-the-century representations of the fallen woman in American literature appear in Stephen Crane's *Maggie: A Girl of the Streets* and Theodore Dreiser's *Sister Carrie*. Each has long been recognized as a work of historical importance in the struggle for a realistic fiction that would deal forthrightly with previously taboo subject matter. Crane's heroine is a girl driven by the poverty of her background into a career as a prostitute, while Dreiser's is a kept woman whose liaisons help her toward a career as a celebrated Broadway actress. ⟨. . .⟩

The reason that *Sister Carrie* was in fact a revolutionary work while *Maggie* was not can be found in the opposite ways in which Dreiser and Crane employed certain fictional formulae while discarding others and also in the two writers' different backgrounds. *Maggie* breaks new American ground in its subject matter: the filth and degradation of the slums, the socially destructive effects of alcoholism, the demimonde of the hooker. The novella appears to be a bold new step toward the liberation of American literature because of the relatively realistic veneer that Crane applies to its seamy surfaces.

Although Crane incongruously began the book while a fraternity man at Syracuse University, he did research his subject in some depth. While still in Syracuse, for example, he investigated the red-light district and interviewed some of its prostitutes. When he arrived in New York a few months later, he began roaming the Bowery, testing the characters and situations in the most recent draft of his story against reality. He became a dedicated observer of the denizens of the down-and-out district, resolving to make his study "sincere," a quality he judged to be missing from earlier nonfictional accounts which had not begun to suggest the horror of the squalid conditions, the brutality, or the tragedy of the wasted lives.

He set about gathering impressions in the manner of the notebook naturalist, sleeping in shelters with derelicts, standing in blizzard-buffeted bread lines, absorbing the dialect. But this was synthetic experience, not preordained by circumstances. Unlike Dreiser, Crane came from a background that was genteel though far from affluent. Crane's father was a respected Methodist minister, and his influence on his son can be observed in the moral assumptions that color the novelist's judgments in *Maggie*. Although Crane rejected the romantic settings and situations in the fiction of his time, he had no quarrel with the formulae that placed beautiful young women on pedestals, rued the effects of demon rum, or, finally and fatally for the novella, punished women who dared to use their bodies to survive the maelstrom of the city.

Maggie opens with a graphic scene designed to make the reader see the reality of Bowery life: gangs bent on establishing one of their own as king of the mountain, in this case a "heap of gravel." Among the urchins, we meet Maggie's brother Jimmie, an aspiring tough who already has developed the "chronic sneer of ideal manhood," the badge of Bowery courage which is validated when he falls to fighting with the members of his own gang near the end of the scene. After Jimmie is dragged home by his father, Crane introduces a description of uncompromising domestic violence behind the "gruesome doorway" of the Johnsons' house. After Jimmie hits Maggie for suggesting that he fights too much, he is pummeled by his mother, both parents engage in a "lurid altercation," and the father, annoyed by the intoxicated condition of his wife, leaves the house bent on a "vengeful drunk."

—Lawrence E. Hussman Jr., "The Fate of the Fallen Woman in *Maggie* and *Sister Carrie*." In *The Image of the Prostitute in Modern Literature*, Frederick Ungar Publishing Co., Inc. (1984): pp. 91–93.

SYDNEY J. KRAUSE ON NATURALISM

[Sydney J. Krause is the author of "Brockden Brown's Feminism in Fact and Fiction" (2000) and "Harold Frederic and the Failure Motif" (1987). In the excerpt below from his article, "The Surrealism of Crane's Naturalism in *Maggie*," Krause discusses the issue of a strict and absolute naturalism which places the story in a highly parodic and modern context.]

The source of Maggie's plight is that her lack of toughness unfits her to withstand the animal callousness of real-life experience. Traumatized by betrayal in love and rejection at home, she sinks into psychic paralysis. In Crane's day, it was his subject that troubled readers; in ours, it is his method. ⟨. . .⟩ Agreeing with those who suggest that the novel is rich and complex in its simplicity, I would like to explore manifestations of one quality that underlies the complexity—namely, the mechanism whereby the naturalistic, when pushed to deformity, acquires an aspect of surrealism, its negative phase portrayed in the triumph of the absurd. As will become apparent, the story is in this sense very modern.

Like its near neighbor satire, surrealism thrives on disparity, situations in which life begins to parody itself. Normal perceptions suddenly arrange themselves in strange and inexplicable relationships, as with French symbolism, German expressionism, Dadaism. Hallucination passes for reality and vice-versa. This becomes the very medium of Maggie's life. From the outset, she is an infantile fantasizer: "Under the trees of her dream-gardens there had always walked a lover." Though they are innocuous enough for a child, when her dreamworld evasions assume an unchanging pattern, one finds Maggie holding on to a schizoid detachment from sordid reality that will make her a prisoner of its horror. The images of tenderness accent her acute vulnerability, as in the over-quoted one of her having "blossomed in a mud puddle" or of her placing a flower in the dead baby's "waxen hand." Tottering on "small legs" and easy to cry, Maggie is frailty personified. Her cover is that of some primitive species which blends in with its natural setting; she is "disguised" by "dirt," "unseen" beneath the "tatters and grime," or leaning "back in the shadow"—until her attractiveness emerges and she is exposed. But a greater danger is the incongruity of Maggie's having thoughts that float off in search of "far away lands where, as God says, the little hills sing together in the morning," while she is physically seated amidst "[t]he broken furniture, grimey walls, and general disorder and dirt of her home"—all of which takes on a merely "potential aspect" (i.e., a pseudopresence—).

Part of Maggie's problem stems from the inordinate fakeries of the world around her, glimpsed in such routine details as the collars she turns out in that room of "twenty girls" with "various shades of yellow discontent." The dislocated collars—to begin with, never seen in natural attachment to shirts—had a name "whose brand could be noted for its irrelevancy to anything in connection with collars." Quite as much as anything else, though, the problem is Maggie herself. Isolated in the cocoon of her naivete, she will insist on romanticizing Pete, her opulent "knight," who, as she sees him, must undoubtedly live "in a blare of pleasure." Thus, perhaps the first thing to be acknowledged is that, whatever its other ingredients, the melodramatic is a blatant property of Maggie's subjectivity gone wild and a point of view, therefore, from which Crane represents the queasy atmosphere of disorientation. This does not quite mean that Maggie is self-doomed; the self was assuredly acting in revulsion from an environment and its gross circumstances, and, as Crane said, he unequivocally intended to show in this book "that environment is a tremendous thing . . . [that] shapes lives regardless." But this mix—particularly as it comes through technically in *Maggie*— does suggest something about the ambiguity of Crane's naturalism (on the one hand, almost precious and obvious, and, on the other, stark and symbolic).

—Sydney J. Krause, "The Surrealism of Crane's Naturalism in *Maggie*," *American Literary Realism 1870–1910*, vol. 16, no. 2 (Autumn 1983): pp. 253–254.

GEORGE T. NOVOTNY ON CLASSICAL INFLUENCES

[George T. Novotny is the author of "Crane's Maggie: A Girl of the Streets" (1992). In the excerpt below from his article, "Crane's *Maggie, A Girl of the Streets*," Novotny discusses the classical and neo-classical influences in the novella.]

In *The Anger of Stephen Crane: Fiction and the Epic Tradition* (1983), Chester L. Wolford suggests that Crane was a "voracious reader" of the classics, citing elements from Crane's early life that could have led to an acquaintance with the writings of Homer and other classical writers. This view is supported by others and has been discussed in Warren D. Anderson's essay, "Homer and Stephen Crane" (1964), as well as in David Halliburton's *The Color of the Sky: A Study of Stephen Crane* (1989). In his book, Wolford examines the possibility of a classical influence in some of Crane's best-known works, including *Maggie, A Girl of the Streets* (1893), Crane's first story.

In reading *Maggie,* I was struck by one passage that recalled a line from Pope's *Dunciad.* In reference to Pete, Maggie's swaggering bartender lover who later discards her, Nell, the "woman of brilliance and audacity," refers to him with the Homeric epithet "my cloud-compelling Pete." Pope, who translated the *Iliad* from 1715 to 1720, also uses the phrase to describe the goddess Dulness in *The Dunciad* (1743): "All these, and more, the cloud-compelling Queen / Beholds thro' fogs, that magnify the scene." Pope's allusion serves to cast Dulness in the role of a sort of anti-Jove.

The *OED* attributes the earliest use of the phrase "cloud-compeller" to the *Iliad,* in Pope's translation, where it is an epithet for Jove: "The cloud compeller, overcome, / Assents to fate, and ratifies the doom." ⟨...⟩

Pete, already feeling increasingly hemmed in by his relationship with Maggie, suffers further ridicule to his fragile ego from Nell, the "woman of brilliance and audacity."

> "A little pale thing with no spirit," she said. "Did you note
> the expression of her eyes? There was something in them
> about pumpkin pie and virtue. That is a peculiar way the
> left corner of her mouth has of twitching, isn't it? Dear,
> dear, my cloud-compelling Pete, what are you coming to?"

One reading of the passage might involve a double irony. On one level, Nell can be seen as deriding Pete for being interested in the slum girl, Maggie. Her use of "cloud-compelling" ridiculously empowers Pete with the Jovian attributes of "mover-and-shaker" that he clearly does not possess. In this sense, Nell is mocking Pete without his awareness.

In a second sense, by figuratively casting Pete in the role of Jove, Crane may well be drawing on a background in the classics to hint to the reader that Maggie's fate is somewhat dependent on the actions of the "cloud-compellers."

In the *Iliad*, Jove wishes to save his son, the demigod Sarpedon, from death at the hands of Patroclus. Juno, however, stays his interference by reminding him that to do so would be to invite meddling by the other gods on behalf of their offspring. Unlike Jove, however, Pete, as "cloud-compeller," cares solely for his own position and "place." Where Jove is deeply pained by the coming loss of his son, yet bows to the exigencies of the greater good, Pete's pain is from his imagined loss of face in the eyes of Nell. Maggie is sacrificed to a greater evil, the brutality of the streets. It might even be possible to extend the comparison to include Nell, as Juno, to Pete's Jove.

In the *Iliad*, as Jove considers aiding Sarpedon, Juno speaks.

> Then thus the goddess with the radiant eyes:
> "What words are these, O sovereign of the skies!
> Short is the date prescribed to mortal man;
> Shall Jove for one extend the narrow span,
> Whose bounds were fix'd before his race began?"

Just as the "goddess with the radiant eyes" counsels Jove against interference with what is determined, the "woman of brilliance and audacity" in effect counsels Pete to leave Maggie to her fate. ⟨. . .⟩

—George T. Novotny, "Crane's *Maggie, A Girl of the Streets*," *The Explicator* 50, no. 4 (Summer 1992): pp. 225–227.

ALICE HALL PETRY ON CRANE'S FAMILIARITY WITH THE ART WORLD

[Alice Hall Petry is the author of "Herbert and Emerson: Emerson's Debt to Herbert" (1987) and "In the Name of the Self: Cather's *The Professor's House*" (1987). In the excerpt below from her article, "*Gin Lane* in the Bowery: Crane's Maggie and William Hogarth," Petry discusses the novella from a particular school of critical commentators who rely on Crane's familiarity with the art world, specifically William Hogarth's depiction of slum life and intemperance.]

Maggie is a tease. For decades now, literary historians and Crane scholars have attempted to ascertain the sources of this painful rendering of late nineteenth-century Bowery slum life, but the results have been far from conclusive. ⟨. . .⟩

This caveat is especially prominent in the commentaries of the other school of *Maggie* source-hunters, those who assume the painterly approach. Drawing upon the incontrovertible facts that Crane's sister Mary Helen was a practicing artist and art instructor; that one of Crane's early loves (approximately 1888 to 1892) was Phebe English, a professional painter; that Crane lived in the studios of several New York illustrators in the 1890s; and that several of his writings—including *The Third Violet*, "The Silver Pageant," and "Stories Told by an Artist"—focus specifically on artists, these commentators argue persuasively that "Crane's involvement with painting . . . seems circumambient in his life." The simple fact that Crane was personally quite familiar with the art world has generated several theories dealing with the ways in which various painterly techniques and movements might have affected the content or style of his fiction or, more broadly, his personal aesthetic. ⟨. . .⟩ One hundred years later, critics such as James Nagel and Sergio Perosa continue, with provocative results, to explore Crane's fiction from the standpoint of Impressionist painting. *Maggie* has had its share of Impressionistic readings; but I think it would be more fruitful to approach that grim tale not from the standpoint of the nineteenth-century French Impressionists but rather from that of the eighteenth-century English Realists. Specifically, I believe that an important pictorial source for Maggie was the famous 1751 engraving *Gin Lane*, by painter/illustrator William Hogarth (1697–1764). ⟨. . .⟩

⟨. . .⟩ It seems far more likely that the name "Rum Alley" was directly inspired by the name "Gin Lane" and/or by the name of the companion-piece of this engraving, "Beer Street" (1751)—Hogarth's paean to the virtues of mild English ale. Even Gullason's reference to Riis points ultimately to Hogarth, for the English engraver's work had inspired a popular volume entitled *Low-Life: or, One Half of the World, knows not how the Other Half lives*, privately printed some time in the 1750s. Crane himself denied to Arthur Bartlett Maurice that he knew the precise location of Rum Alley, but avowed that he "had seen" it and that it "had haunted him and still haunted him."

Might he not have been "haunted" (consciously or otherwise) by the memory of Hogarth's nightmare vision of Augustan London—a vision which bore startling resemblance to the Bowery of the 1890s?

Both visions, after all, focus on two issues which touched Crane deeply: slum life and intemperance. *Maggie* is now regarded as the first American novel to depict urban slum life artistically, and Hogarth's engravings performed a comparable service for eighteenth-century London—so much so that a controversy arose as to whether unpalatable engravings such as *Gin Lane* even qualified as art. Charles Dickens himself was struck by the degree to which *Gin Lane* "forces on [our] attention a most neglected [,] wretched neighbour-hood, and an unwholesome, indecent [,] abject condition of life"—words which could just as readily be applied to *Maggie*. More to the point, much of the misery depicted in both Crane's and Hogarth's works is directly attributable to the vicious cycle of poverty and readily-available cheap liquor. *Gin Lane* was Hogarth's personal contribution to the prohibition movement in eighteenth-century England, and in fact *Gin Lane* was credited with bringing about the so-called Tippling Act, designed to curtail the sale of liquor in the British Isles.

—Alice Hall Petry, "*Gin Lane* in the Bowery: Crane's *Maggie* and William Hogarth," *American Literature* 56, no. 3 (October 1984) pp. 417–420.

Karen E. Waldron on the Journalistic Style

[Karen E. Waldron is the author of "Coming to Consciousness, Coming to Voice: The Reinvention of Eve in American Women's Writings" (1994). In the excerpt below from her article, "No Separations in the City: The Public-Private Novel and Private-Public Authorship," Waldron discusses the issue of literary representation versus realism in Crane's journalistically-styled story of *Maggie: A Girl of the Streets*.]

⟨. . .⟩ As Amy Kaplan notes, realist fiction documents a need to determine what *is* real in a world of striking class differences set next to mass discursive culture. Thus realism "explores and bridges the perceived gap between the social world and literary representation" through the relation of narrator and text. The outsider, viewing an environment, makes the realist author akin to the journalist who could be directed by Greeley's editorial nativism or Fuller's related sense of the newspapers' formal potential. Certainly works focusing on cities and gender like Howells's *The Rise of Silas Lapham,* James's *The Bostonians,* and Phelps's *The Silent Partner* all highlight the conflict between perceived public and private identities with subtextual analyses of journalistic representation.

Stephen Crane, however, like Fern and Davis, explicitly merged fictional and journalistic techniques through his narrative position. He also resisted idealizing tendencies with an emphasis on environmental determinism. While realism was yet forming as a self-conscious mode of fictional representation, the tension between idealistic and naturalistic goals, dramatized by continuing debates over the cause and reality of private and public lives, began manifesting the contradictions of realism as narrative and representational system. Kaplan's, Brodhead's, and Lang's work, alongside Crane's own essay "Howells Fears Realists Must Wait" (1894; reprinted in Stallman, *Omnibus*), suggest these tensions arise at least in part out of conflicting discourses of domesticity, private and public spheres, gender, regionalism, mass culture, and nationalism that the public-private journalistic novel exposes. Crane's *Maggie: A Girl of the Streets* moves the insights of *Ruth Hall* and *Life in the Iron Mills* about the discourse of separate spheres to a city where even the hope that *Life in the Iron Mills* ends with— marked, significantly, by "clover-crimsoned meadows," "long years of sunshine, and fresh air"—disappears. Maggie's is an expanded and isolating urban world that makes mockery of "natural" gender inclinations, domesticity, and the presumed purity of private life. There are no separations possible in the city *Maggie* details, and none through either narrative personae (as with Fern's pseudonym) or narrative interpretation (the Christian pastoral rhetoric of *Life in the Iron Mills*). As a result, there is no way for the female protagonist to outlast her text, as Ruth and Deborah eventually did, by moving finally into a privatized domesticity deriving from separate male and female, work and home, city and country, and/or public and private spheres.

Crane subordinates the ideological work of gender in *Maggie* to the power of an urban environment under the influence of mass culture along with increasing immigration, poverty, and industrialization. No longer are concerns of class veiled in a voyeuristic peering into the city; the tentative experiences of the character Ruth Hall and Davis's narrator, the need to frame stories with a private-public authorial identity that claims simultaneous identification with and the power to describe and categorize the other (as perceived significantly not by gender but class, ethnicity, physical location and economic status), disappears. Embedded in the third-person point of view of the text, the narrator's presumed familiarity with such different spheres manifests as a matter of style rather than proclamation. *Maggie* textualizes as narrative consciousness, not narrative voice, a realism that declines the idealistic and egoistic tendency to overtly highlight the mind and presence of the private-public writer. As the city becomes the authorial vehicle, transforming the center of consciousness to the fictional text that implies but does not speak of its author, realism's discursive paradoxes evolve.

—Karen E. Waldron, "Narrative Fiction as Separation? Stephen Crane's *Maggie*, and the Logistics of Realism, and Gender in the City." In *Separate Spheres No More: Gender Convergence in American Literature, 1830–1930*, Elbert, Monika M., ed. (Tuscaloosa and London: The University of Alabama Press, 2000): pp. 104–106.

Plot Summary of
The Red Badge of Courage

In **Chapter I** we are introduced to the young Henry Fleming as he awakens on the banks of a river, amidst "the retiring fogs," and to Henry's friend, Jim Conklin, who rushes back to his regiment to report that he just overheard the news that the regiment would be engaged in battle by the next day. And, as the other men in this squad are inexperienced, much excitement is aroused by this news, especially in the young protagonist, Henry Fleming, who has a very romantic concept of war and the honors bestowed on the heroic warrior. "The youth was in a trance of astonishment. . . . [t]hat he was about to mingle in one of those great affairs of the earth." Indeed, Henry wonders whether his comrades can achieve the glory of ancient Greek warriors. "He had long despaired of witnessing a Greeklike struggle. Such would be no more. . . ." Indeed, it is from this romantic ideal that Henry was inspired to enlist in the first place, though he remembers his mother's words as she tried to dissuade her son. "She had affected to look with some contempt upon the quality of his war ardor and patriotism" and promises to continue her life whether or not he ever returns. Henry also begins to wonder about his own success in battle and those aspects of his character which have not yet been tested, namely his courage and bravery when his very life would be at stake. "He tried to mathematically prove to himself that he would not run from battle."

Nevertheless, in the **first two chapters**, while Henry continues to worry about his own courage, there is a feeling of monotony and frustration as the soldiers learn that they are not about to move. And the following night finds an increasingly exhausted regiment marching along a shore, with "a dark and mysterious range of hills," though the enemy fails to appear. However, one morning Henry is rudely awakened by Jim Conklin to the sound of distant gunfire. At this point, as the regiment begins to run, they take on the characteristics of a stampede, maneuvering past the body of a dead soldier, a scene which evokes another poignancy and reality about the nature of battle and the lives of the actual combatants, all of which run counter to Henry's heretofore romantic notions. "It was as if fate had betrayed the solider. In death it exposed to his enemies that poverty which in life he had perhaps concealed from this friends." In the next chapter, as the regiment stops in a grove with the chaos of battle raging around them, a group of enemy soldiers stampedes towards them.

In **Chapter V**, Henry's regiment is attacked and the men begin to fire back with the captain shouting instructions from behind. Here, Henry's sense of individuality is transformed into a recognition that he is now a single cog in a machine. "He became not a man but a member. . . . He was welded into a common personality which was dominated by a single desire." As the battle continues, a rage overtakes the other men who burst forth in a "wild, barbaric song" while another soldier attempts to flee, only to be beaten by the lieutenant. When the battle is over, Henry notices that the sun is shining and that Nature continues to maintain her own course despite the carnage that is taking place. "It was surprising that Nature had gone tranquilly on with her golden process in the midst of so much devilment." And, these revelations will continue in **Chapter VI,** as Henry loses some of his romantic notions. "A lad whose face had borne an expression of exalted courage. . . . [b]lanched like one who has come to the edge of a cliff at midnight and is suddenly made aware." Indeed, it is equally significant that our young soldier begins to recognize that his own success in battle might be measured in how swiftly he can flee, an act which will cause him a great deal of self-recrimination through much of the narrative until he can successfully prove himself a valiant solider. "In his flight the sound of these following footsteps gave him his one meager relief. . . . So he displayed the zeal of an insane sprinter in his purpose to keep them in the rear. There was a race." He has forgotten his part in the vast machine of war, and returns to his overwhelming concern for individual self-preservation. "The youth turned to look behind him and off to the right and off to the left. He experienced the joy of a man who at last finds leisure in which to look about him."

In **Chapter VII**, while walking alone in the forest, Henry is feeling guilt about have fled the battlefield, "cring[ing] as if discovered in a crime." At the same time, he is very disturbed by the thought that there are other soldiers, those in his regiment who remained to defeat the enemy without his help. "He, the enlightened man . . . had fled because of his superior perceptions and knowledge. . . . He knew it could be proved that they had been fools." Deep into the woods and far from battle, Henry begins to rationalize his actions and find consolation in nature. "This landscape gave him assurance. . . . He conceived Nature to be a woman with a deep aversion to tragedy." But Henry soon discovers that he has not completely escaped the ravages of the battlefield as he stumbles upon the dead body of a soldier in a tattered blue uniform, "[t]he eyes, staring at the youth, had changed to the dull hue to be seen on the side of a dead fish." It is a very grim and shocking experience to come face to face with the reality of death. "The youth gave a shriek as he confronted the thing. He was for moments turned to stone." In **Chapter VIII**, Henry is trying to make his way through the forest where, hearing "the crimson roar" of fighting, he is brought back to the reality of war. "The battle was like the grinding of an immense and terrible machine to him." It is here that Henry meets up with another group of wounded men and among them is the tattered man who appears like a walking corpse. The tattered soldier will soon ask Henry the very uncomfortable and embarrassing questions of how he has been wounded. Henry's response is to run away suddenly as he "slid through the crowd." And, in so doing, Henry enters another critical juncture as he becomes envious of the physical signs of their bravery in the wounded men around him. "He conceived persons with torn bodies to be peculiarly happy. He wished that he, too, had a wound, a red badge of courage." Shortly thereafter, he discovers his injured friend, Jim Conklin, and promises to take care of him, though Jim orders Henry not to come near him. And, when Henry and the tattered man witness Jim's collapse and demise, Henry becomes enraged at the sight. "The youth turned, with sudden, livid rage, toward the battlefield. He shook his fist. He seemed about to deliver a philippic." And in this reference to the philippic, a formal and war-like declamation, full of eloquence and acrimony, we are given yet another ironic comparison between the heroic language of ancient Greece and the language of Henry Fleming's world where the idiom of all the men around is comprised of local dialect.

In the **following few chapters**, Henry's guilt and feelings of wretchedness for having acted so cowardly are intensified as he watches other soldiers return from battle. "[T]he black weight of woe returned to him. . . . The separation was as great to him as if they had marched with weapons of flame and banners of sunlight. . . . He could have wept in his longings." However, Henry has no rifle, he is hungry and thirsty, and is therefore in no condition to engage the enemy. Since he does not believe that that soldiers in blue will lose, Henry tries fabricating a story that will excuse his cowardly behavior, but does not succeed even in this attempt. His imagination simply fails to alleviate or transform his feelings into consolation. "In imagination he felt the scrutiny of his companions as he painfully labored through some lies." In **Chapter XII**, Henry finally receives the much coveted injury, and sign of bravery, that he has so longed for when he receives a bloody wound to his head, iron-ically from another fleeing soldier. However, this too does not bring a feeling of vindication, for it is merely an outward sign. "The little blistering voices of pain that had called out from his scalp were, he thought, definite in their expression of danger. By them he believed that he could measure his plight." At this point, a well-intentioned stranger appears and helps Henry find his way back to his company.

However, the help of the stranger brings only further cause for unhappiness as Henry is anxious lest the other men in his regiment make him into a pariah for having fled from battle. "He had a con-viction that he would soon feel in his sore heart the barbed missiles of ridicule." And, as he wends his way past his sleeping comrades, a loud voice shouts at him to stop. It is Wilson. Henry explains that he has been shot by another regiment. Wilson nurses the young Henry Fleming, tending to his wounds with a canteen of coffee, a wet cloth and a blanket for the night. As Henry awakens to a misty dawn in **Chapter XIV**, he realizes that there has been a great change in his friend. Wilson is no longer loud but, rather, has become quiet and remarkably confident. "There was about him now a fine reliance. He showed a quiet belief in his purposes and his abilities." And, although Henry does not yet realize this, it is Wilson's inner confi-dence which is the true mark and achievement of a brave soldier. At this point in the narrative, **Chapter XV**, Henry is still petrified of having his cowardice exposed, and thus we see him continuing to cling to whatever exculpatory evidence he can lay hold of, such as the yellow envelope that Wilson wanted him to deliver to his family in the event of his death. "But he had not died, and thus he had delivered himself into the hands of this youth." For Henry, the enve-lope has the symbolic power to save him from being caught in a lie.

In the **concluding chapters**, however, Henry Fleming is presented with the opportunity to redeem himself in two very important ways. Both Henry and Wilson overhear their regiment being insulted by enemy commanders, one of whom refers to them as a group of "mule drivers" who do not stand a chance of winning. The two men, dismayed by the news and with firm resolve to prepare their comrades for the impending battle, they refrain from telling the other men what they have heard, lest they become disheartened. But, most importantly, Henry Fleming does exhibit true courage and valor in battle. "He himself felt the daring spirit of a savage, religion-mad. He was capable of profound sacrifices, a tremendous death." And, both he and Wilson receive commendation from one of the officers. This praise gives Henry a feeling of pride, "a serene self-confidence," that he is now in fact a brave soldier. And, finally, in the concluding chapter, the psychological war of emotions, most especially the painfully irrepressible memory of his former cowardice, that has been raging inside himself is finally put into perspective with the promise of having newly-discovered abilities to work it out. "There was in him a creed of freedom which no contemplation of inexorable law could destroy. He saw himself living in watchfulness, frustrating the plans of the unchangeable, making of fate a fool."

First published in book form in late September 1895 by D. Appleton & Co., *The Red Badge of Courage* is considered to be a masterpiece of American literature. However, its more immediate success is in early 1896 in England where critics hail Stephen Crane to be a literary genius. In January 1896, The London *Bookman* praised the realism of Crane's depiction of the civil war, and the London *Saturday Review* recommended the novel to its readers as "the most realistic description ever published of modern war." Given that the Civil War was still a somewhat recent memory in this country, the American reviews were mixed. In referring to Crane's symbolic use of color, the *New York Tribune* dubbed the novel a "chromatic nightmare" that was "devoid of tragic power," while the *Detroit Free Press,* in comparing Crane's writing style to that of Victor Hugo, stated that *The Red Badge of Courage* "will give you so vivid a picture of the emotions and the horrors of the battlefield that you will pray your eyes may never look upon the reality," and the *New York Times* praised Crane for his portrayal of war as "extraordinarily true," while stating that his writing needed tone and discipline.

All of the contemporary reviews notwithstanding, however, Crane's masterpiece must also be understood within the context of the 1890s and the audience whom he was addressing. In the last critical decade of the nineteenth century, the nation was experiencing the dawn of a new era. While the America of the past had been rural, individualistic and expansionary, the social reality that was beginning to take hold was that of an urban-centered and industrialized world where the focus on the individual was lost in the overcrowded slums and sweatshops that were contributing to a new economy of mass production made possible through a great influx of immigrant labor alongside many scientific and technological advances. It was also the age that saw the Homestead Steel Strike, the Antitrust Act and the formation of the Populist Party. From a critical standpoint, it is important to note that from the very outset, several descriptive literary terms have been used to define Crane's work, first and foremost applying the term naturalism to his work. Naturalism is often an ambiguous term which can refer to a romantic description of nature or, with respect to Stephen Crane, identifying a highly specific aesthetic principle which is decidedly unromantic in its belief that man's existence is a constant struggle for life subordinate to the laws of rapacious destiny in which nature's benign aspects are in sharp contrast to the human experience. Indeed, the young Henry Fleming leaves both his mother and the peaceful yet uninspiring rural way of life to enlist in the army for what at first promised to be the romantic life of a soldier. And it is no small detail that his mother soon becomes resigned to her son's choice and, after her parting words of advice to act with honor and integrity, her presence in the text quickly recedes. "There's lots of bad men in the army, Henry. . . . Keep clear of them folks, Henry. I don't want yeh to ever do anything, Henry, that yeh would be 'shamed to let me know about."

Henry Fleming experiences this sharp contrast throughout the novel where Nature is sympathetic to his innermost aversion to war yet, at the same time, unable to rescue him from the grim reality in which he must survive. "The swishing saplings tried to make known his presence to the world. He could not conciliate the forest. As he made his way, it was always calling out protestations." In fact, Nature becomes problematic because it has the potential to expose Henry Fleming's presence and, thus, his cowardice after having run away from his regiment. Furthermore, with respect to a view of a sympathetic nature which can no longer provide hope and consolation to the battle weary, nature and man are both symbolically gendered. Henry Fleming "conceived Nature to be a woman with a deep aversion to tragedy," while he must struggle to survive the masculine battlefield which is described throughout the novel as "the grinding of an immense and terrible machine" of "grim processes" which "produce corpses." Indeed, the many associations of war in *The Red Badge of Courage* with the mechanical locate this text within the context of scientific and mechanistic determinism which marks late nineteenth century America. "The torn bodies expressed the awful machinery in which the men had been entangled" while another traumatized soldier in Henry's company is described as moving "mechanically, dully, with his animal-like eyes upon the officer" and whose shaking hands could no longer reload his gun. Indeed, even the lieutenant has thought deeply about "the science of war."

Finally, another descriptive term for Nature and which applies to Stephen Crane's writing style is that of literary impressionism. Impressionism is an aesthetic term which originally applied to a style of painting and defined an entire artistic movement in Europe during the late nineteenth century. As a style of painting, impressionism demonstrates how our perception of Nature is a succession of fleeting images due to the constantly changing effects of reflected sunlight on the objects being observed. Although the artists which made up this movement were highly individual and differentiated from one another, they all experimented with bold primary colors rendered with brushstrokes of dabs or tiny dots. Their aim was to simulate actual reflected light. As a literary style, impressionism depicts a scene or emotion by the use of detail that is brief yet essential, and is intended to create vividness of mood and a memorable impression. Instances of impressionism abound within *The Red Badge of Courage*. At times, the sunlight offers a magnificent view of nature. "Gray mists were slowly shifting before the first efforts of the sun rays. An impending splendor could be seen in the eastern sky." But the ravages of war stand in sharp contrast to the beauty of nature, and the images formed in light of day, although memorable, are not a celebration of the present moment, but rather produce an intense feeling of alienation and dislocation of the self. "Swift pictures of himself, apart, yet in himself, came to him—a blue desperate figure leading lurid charges with one knee forward and a broken blade high—a blue, determined figure standing before a crimson and steel assault. . . ." Indeed, Henry Fleming has trouble placing himself amidst the scene of death and destruction. Furthermore, the brilliant though often lurid images of Henry Fleming's perception are in sharp contrast to instances of other young soldiers "blanching" in fear of death who, only moments earlier were brave in appearance, "[a] lad whose face had borne an expression of exalted courage" now "blanched like one who has come to the edge of a cliff at midnight and is suddenly made aware. There was a revelation. He, too, threw down his gun and fled." The rapid transformation of Henry Fleming's perception of this young man from bravery to cowardice is yet a further instance of an impressionistic moment wherein our perceptions are subject to both rapid and radical change and appearances are fleeting and untrustworthy.

But Henry is determined nevertheless. "He had burned several times to enlist. Tales of great movements shook the land. They might not be distinctly Homeric, but there seemed to be much glory in them." Henry was soon to find out differently. Having revealed his early and wholly inexperienced romantic notions of war, it is important to note that Henry Fleming's Homeric references are scattered throughout the text and have also been part of the critical debate about *The Red Badge of Courage.* This debate is about the epic tradition, specifically that of ancient Greece where this genre was of paramount importance. The epic in terms of Homer's *Odyssey* is a long narrative poem that treats of heroic figures and their relationship with the Greek gods, the part they play in an historical event; their behavior is measured in a society's perception of virtuous conduct.

The epic is also considered a pseudo-historical document which plays an important role in remembering and recounting a nation's history. However, in the case of *The Red Badge of Courage,* historical details are almost entirely absent and reference to the American Civil War is extremely sketchy. Indeed, the most important battle that takes place in this novel is in the psychological arena of Henry's mind and the ways in which he struggles with issues of courage, manhood, the meaning of life and the need to be mindful of his own self-preservation. While the novel begins with Henry's romantic notions, based on a hero of ancient Greece who was welcomed back with praise, his mother advises him to act with honesty and integrity above all other motivations. Henry also begins with the expectation that his military experience will earn him the admiration of women and respect of other men, though by the end of the story he understands the true test of manhood is the far less "romantic" concept of fulfilling one's obligations. And, finally, after stumbling upon the corpse of another solider, Henry begins to recognize that death is but an unremarkable fact of nature and human life.

It is also very interesting to note from the very start that although this novel takes place during the American Civil War, very little historical context is provided, and when it does mention some particular historical detail, it is usually quite subtle, as is illustrated in the first few paragraphs of the novel in the description of a black man amongst the Union soldiers. "A negro teamster who had been dancing upon a cracker box with hilarious encouragement of two score soldiers was deserted. He sat mournfully down." There is a great poignancy in the plight of this black workingman whose presence can be so easily effaced in so short an interval of time, with the suggestion that he is grieving for his own loss of identity, an unjust fate which he shares with the slaves of the South.

Equally important in Homer is the idea that his heroes are acting out a predetermined fate and central to the portrayal of the hero is his success in action which will further buttress his reputation. Critical commentary on the genre of epic poetry has also identified the role of invention which here is equated with a sustained brilliant imagination concerning the action, the speeches of the characters and the description of the natural world. The epic, as well as all the other ancient Greek poetic and dramatic genres, invoked the help of the various mythological gods. In *The Red Badge of Courage,* these powerful gods have been rendered powerless and ineffectual. "Strange gods were addressed in condemnation of the early hours necessary to correct war. An officer's peremptory tenor rang out and quickened the stiffened movement of the men. The tangled limbs unraveled. The corpse-hued faces were hidden behind fists that twisted slowly in eye sockets."

Finally, another important feature of the *Odyssey,* as well as other great epics that followed, namely Virgil's *Aeneid* and the *Inferno* of Dante's *Divine Comedy,* affords the hero a view of the underworld under the benevolent supervision of a guide, with the expectation of increased understanding of the importance of leading a virtuous life and the consequences for not doing so. Indeed, along these lines of a hero's education, there is also critical debate as to whether *The Red Badge of Courage* is a bildungsroman, a story about the coming of age and spiritual education of its main character, Henry Fleming. All of these points regarding the epic have a bearing on our interpretation of *The Red Badge of Courage* and, in many instances, take on a very ironic or incongruous significance when compared to their epic analogues. ❀

List of Characters in
The Red Badge of Courage

Henry Fleming—the novel's young protagonist and a young soldier fighting for the Union army during the American Civil War. At first, Henry is inexperienced in battle and questions his own courage. Later on he experiences the war and struggles with the universe's indifference to existence and his own life. While holding very romantic notions at the outset, yet fleeing from battle at first, he later becomes a real solider in combat.

Jim Conklin, Henry's friend who is injured during the regiment's first battle and dies shortly thereafter of his wounds. Early on in the narrative, Jim provides a moral contrast to Henry.

Wilson, a loud person in the regiment and a friend of Henry. Wilson and Henry grow close as they share the harsh experiences of war and later earn the reputation as their regiment's best soldiers.

The Tattered Soldier, a soldier whom Henry encounters in a column of wounded men. With his constant speculation about Henry's wound, he becomes Henry's nagging and painful conscience.

The Lieutenant, a youthful officer and Henry's commander in battle, given over to profuse swearing during battle. When Henry gains the reputation of a brave soldier, he and the lieutenant develop a bond for one another, recognizing that they must work together to motivate the other men.

Henry's Mother, has a very limited role in a flashback at the beginning of the narrative. Though Henry enlists despite her protests, Henry continues to struggle with her objections and admonitions about the meaning of an individual life within the greater scheme of the world. ❀

Critical Views on
The Red Badge of Courage

JEAN R. HALLADAY ON CARLYLEAN ECHOES

[Jean R. Halladay is the author of "*Sartor Resartus* Revisited: Carlylean Echoes in Crane's *The Red Badge of Courage*." In the excerpt below from that article, Halladay discusses the intertextual relationship between these two literary works by suggesting that Henry Fleming's ordeal and eventual triumph is a reenactment of Carlyle's characterization of Diogenes Teufelsrockh.]

That the writings of Thomas Carlyle have been widely influential is, of course, a truism. A reader with a close knowledge of Carlyle often finds echoes of him in unexpected places in the works of others. An example of this may be seen in the works of Stephen Crane. A close examination of *The Red Badge of Courage* side by side with the "Everlasting No"—"Everlasting Yea" chapters from *Sartor Resartus* leaves a reader with the impression that Henry Fleming's ordeal and eventual triumph in the *Red Badge* may well be a kind of subconscious reenactment of the ordeal and triumph of Diogenes Teufelsdrockh in that central portion of *Sartor Resartus*.

While it cannot be proven on the basis of presently available evidence that Crane had read any of Carlyle's works, the possibility of his having done so exists. In the one semester, in 1891, that Crane spent at Syracuse University, the only course for which he received a grade was "English Literature," in which he made an "A". *Sartor Resartus* had been directly available to American readers since its American publication in 1836. ⟨. . .⟩ In my own teaching of Carlyle, I have repeatedly observed the powerful impression that these two Sartor passages make upon students' minds—particularly young students. Because of this, I believe it possible that Carlyle's ideas could have remained in Crane's mind long after he had consciously forgotten about reading them. If this possibility is true then it is further possible that some of these ideas made their way into the *Red Badge*. Whatever the cause—subconscious influence, coincidence, Zeitgeist—the similarities between the two works do exist. They include not only similarities in situation, but parallel

52

passages, similarities in phrasing, and the use of like images in like situations. Also, with few exceptions, the order in which these parallels occur is the same in the two works.

The initial similarities between the two works center around the early stages of the ordeal of each of the main characters. "The Everlasting No," Chapter VII of Book II of *Sartor Resartus,* begins with an explanation that Diogenes Teufelsdrockh has been suffering through a period of crisis, or transition in his life, and goes on:

> Such transitions are ever full of pain: thus the Eagle when
> he moults is sickly; and, to attain his new beak, must
> harshly dash-off the old one upon rocks.

In Chapter I of *The Red Badge of Courage,* Henry Fleming, having heard the latest rumors that the army is about to move into combat, goes into his hut to think about the possibility of himself engaged in battle. Like Diogenes, Henry is at the beginning of his period of crisis, and undergoing the same feeling of being disappointed, mocked by destiny. Like Carlyle, Crane here also uses an eagle image in the description of the beginning of the main character's ordeal. "In visions he had seen himself in many struggles. He had imagined peoples secure in the shadow of his eagle-eyed prowess." Before enlisting in the army, Henry had been distrustful of the Civil War, believing it to be a pale imitation of the "Greek like struggle" involved in ancient wars, and yet he had "burned" to enlist. "He had read of marches, sieges, conflicts, and he had longed to see it all." Now with the possibility that actual battle may be imminent, Henry faces the fear that he may be afraid. He feels himself to be "an unknown quantity."

Again, in "The Everlasting No," further describing Diogenes' spiritual crisis, Carlyle writes that the most painful feeling

> . . . is that of your own Feebleness (Unkraft); ever, as the
> English Milton says, to be weak is the true misery. And yet
> of your strength there is and can be no clear feeling, save
> by what you have prospered in, by what you have done.

> —Jean R. Halladay, "*Sartor Resartus* Revisited: Carlylean Echoes in Crane's *The Red Badge of Courage,*" *Nineteenth Century Prose* (Winter 1988/89): pp. 23–24.

HAROLD KAPLAN ON THE CIVIL WAR AS RELIGIOUS REVELATION

[Harold Kaplan is the author of *Conscience and Memory: Meditations in a Museum of the Holocaust* (1994) and *Democratic Humanism and American Literature* (1972). In the excerpt below from his article, "Vitalism and Redemptive Violence," Kaplan discusses the novel in terms of Crane's imagining of the Civil War which he characterizes as a "poetry of violence," leading to a type of religious revelation.]

The naturalist obsession with violence can, when conditioned by an imaginative sensibility and raised to the level of revelation—emerge in the form of ritual observations and ceremonial drama. Stephen Crane had that kind of sensibility, tightening what is loose allegory in Norris, and in *The Red Badge of Courage* he developed a poetry of violence that singles that book out in the mainstream of naturalist fiction.

Crane did not need to know the Civil War personally because he knew it so well imaginatively; all that he needed were the naturalist myths that fed his imagination. His book is powerful, standing out above the works of Norris, London, and even Dreiser, not because it documents the life of camp and battle but because it is highly focused on primitive mysteries in battle and death.

Crane is clearly attempting to give a religious coloring to these revelations. Nature contains a god, and his service is sacrifice and death. War is nature's stormy Mount Sinai, "war, the red animal—war, the blood-swollen god." All that nature contains of great force, pain, death, extreme physical effort, and ultimate physical collapse are given their high ground of revelation in war. It is there that these naturalist truths meet and converge on a metaphysical level. And when Henry Fleming is most absorbed by the battle, he knows war in this way: "He himself felt the daring spirit of a savage, religion—mad. He was capable of profound sacrifices, a tremendous death."

But since Henry is entirely oblivious of the political or moral justifications of this war, his battle crisis reveals only the cosmic processes of survival and death. Here can be found naturalism's nearest approach to religious transcendence, and it occurs at the boundaries of biological fate. And this is the essence of naturalist heroism: to approach the mystery of nature depends on the will to confront its most savage truth, sacrificing a mundane safety. Crane mentions "profound sacrifices," but it is clear that these sacrifices have no specific moral purpose. The value is metaphysical and personal, and the antagonist is not a human being but natural violence and death.

Violence possesses awesome meaning here because it opens toward death. The major confrontation with naturalist mystery is not in battle itself, for it comes to Henry Fleming when he is running away from battle. The scene is described in explicitly religious terms:

> he reached a place where the high, arching boughs made a chapel. He softly pushed the green doors aside and entered. Pine needles were a gentle brown carpet. There was a religious half light.
>
> Near the threshold he stopped, horror-stricken at the sight of a thing.

The "thing" is a dead man, seated with his back against a tree, and the chapel containing that thing expresses the lucid power of Crane's imagination. Crane of course complicates the religious references with the irony that is characteristic of all his writing, but here the irony is complex, not obviously reductive. Nothing of the shock of physical death is withheld; the eyes of the dead man have "the dull hue to be seen on the side of a dead fish," and

> Over the gray skin of the face ran little ants. One was trundling some sort of bundle along the upper lip. ⟨. . .⟩

A fuller initiation into the mystery of death takes place later, in the prolonged agony of Henry's friend, Jim Conklin. As he walks beside Henry in the parade of the wounded, Jim is dying on his feet, staring into the unknown: "he seemed always looking for a place, like one who goes to choose a grave," and, already spectral in his look, he says, "don't tech me—leave me be." The dying man is preparing himself: "there was something ritelike in these movements of the doomed soldier." ⟨. . .⟩

—Harold Kaplan, "Vitalism and Redemptive Violence." In *Power and Order: Henry Adams and the Naturalist Tradition in American Fiction*, (Chicago and London: University of Chicago Press, 1981): pp. 121–123.

[Thomas L. Kent is the author of "The Second Quarto of *Othello* and the Question of Textual Authority" (1991) and "The Classification of Genres" (1983). In the excerpt below from his article, "Epistemological Uncertainty in *The Red Badge of Courage*," Kent discusses the novel as thematizing the tensions accompanying Crane's strict adherence to realistic storytelling.]

From our historical angle of vision, Stephen Crane's ties to traditional nineteenth-century fiction and especially to naturalism seem more aesthetical than metaphysical or ideological. From the naturalistic tradition best represented by Zola, Crane borrows the techniques of close, detailed observation, detached narrative point of view, and irony. But in combination with these devices, Crane also employs a highly charged symbolism that goes beyond the technical formulations elaborated by naturalistic theorists like Zola and Garland about what constitutes an artistic narrative. Crane seems to be at once a symbolist and a naturalist, and the uncertainty about how to read his fiction—about how to distinguish a symbol from the real thing—becomes part of the subject matter of his stories. This kind of aesthetic uncertainty is not the same as the uncertainty generally associated with blind chance, one of the forces like heredity or environment that animates existence in a deterministic universe; rather, the uncertainty encountered in Crane's most successful fiction is epistemological in nature. Commenting about "The Open Boat," Donna Gerstenberger maintains that the tale "may best be viewed as a story with an epistemological emphasis, one which constantly reminds its readers of the impossibility of man's *knowing* anything, even that which he experiences." The "epistemological emphasis" Gerstenberger discovers in "The Open Boat" may be detected as well in *The Red Badge of Courage*. In *The Red Badge of Courage*, Crane confronts a distinctly twentieth-century problem, man's limited ability to know the meaning of existence, and he refuses to endorse without serious reservations any metaphysical precept, any moral or ethical value structure, including determinism.

In *The Red Badge of Courage*, epistemological uncertainty may be seen to function on two levels: on the narrative level within the text where characters and events are interwoven and on the extratextual level, or audience level, where judgments must be made by the reader about the meaning of the text. On the narrative level, the characters who populate *The Red Badge of Courage* are uncertain about their existential condition; they seek continually to know the meaning of events going on around them. On the extratextual level, the reader is uncertain about how to interpret the meaning of the narrative; he continually seeks to know how to "read" the story. In this way, Crane constructs a text that creates epistemological difficulties for the reader on the extratextual level while, at the same time, transforming epistemology on the narrative level into the subject matter of the text. So, in a sense, Crane manages to transform the very structure of the text into its own subject matter. In addition to the epistemological uncertainty that is treated overtly on the narrative and extratextual levels, Crane compounds the reader's difficulty by employing a subtle, mystifying narrator who revels in producing ironic commentary and ambiguous conceits. By suggesting different meanings for events and by manufacturing conceits—like the wafer simile—that have multiple associations and many possible interpretations, the narrator helps increase the reader's uncertainty and perplexity until, finally, this uncertainty and perplexity become, paradoxically, the real "meaning" of the texts.

—Thomas Kent, "Epistemological Uncertainty in the *Red Badge of Courage*," *Modern Fiction Studies* 27, no. 4 (Winter 1981–82): pp. 621–622.

JOHN J. MCDERMOTT ON SYMBOLISM AND PSYCHOLOGICAL REALISM

[John J. McDermott is the author of "From the Other Side of the Furrow: A Folk-Group Sampler" (1986) and "The Landed Heritage of Texas Writing" (1986). In the excerpt below from his article, "Symbolism and Psychological Realism in *The Red Badge of Courage*," McDermott discusses some of the thematic devices Crane uses to create dramatic tension.]

In choosing as protagonist for *The Red Badge of Courage* an unsophisticated, inarticulate farm boy, and in attempting convincingly to depict in this protagonist a complicated, only partially rational, psychological change, Stephen Crane obviously set for himself a task of formidable artistic difficulty. One of the devices he uses to overcome this difficulty is the series of thematically related incidents with which he opens his novel. Together these incidents form an appropriate backdrop against which the drama of Henry Fleming's private struggle for manhood may be presented.

A juxtaposition of no more than the title, *The Red Badge of Courage,* and some opening lines of the work indicates that Crane's novel is enriched with complicating ironies. For the first badge of virtue we see in the novel is a deceptive one: a "tall soldier" (who we later learn is Jim Conklin, the most conventionally courageous soldier in the novel) having "developed virtues," decides, as a first practical result of his new-found virtues, to wash his dirty shirt. While laundering he naively absorbs an inaccurate rumor which he feels compelled to share with his fellows. He then waves his freshly cleaned "banner-like" shirt aloft and rushes back to camp. There he repeats the tale which he has just heard, only to have it immediately and with partial accuracy identified by one of his listeners as "'a thunderin' lie!'" Conventional virtue, then, Crane announces as his work opens, may well lead only to trivial actions, and its flaunted banners may herald only partial truths.

The specific virtue of courage in battle is soon introduced in similarly mocking contexts. Even before the battle begins, veteran soldiers tell Henry Fleming that the enemy may be advancing while "chewing tobacco with unspeakable valor." As the army moves to a confrontation with the enemy, Bill Smithers, one of the men in Henry's regiment, stumbles and falls, and as he lies sprawling one of his own comrades treads on his hand. We later learn Smithers has three fingers crushed so badly by this accident that a doctor wants to amputate them. But at the time of the trampling the rest of the men in the ranks merely laugh as Smithers swears in pain, the first among them to be wounded. And as the regiment continues its march toward the battle lines the men satirically cheer the first opponent they encounter, a "dauntless" young girl who fights with a fat private for possession of her horse: "They jeered the piratical private, and called attention to various defects in his personal appearance; and they were wildly enthusiastic in support of the young girl." So Crane skillfully dramatizes an external reality which challenges the simpleminded notions of heroism which his naive protagonist has brought with him to the army.

—John J. McDermott, "Symbolism and Psychological Realism in *The Red Badge of Courage*," *Nineteenth Century Fiction* 23, no. 3 (December 1968): pp. 324–325.

JAMES NAGEL ON LITERARY IMPRESSION

[James Nagel is the author of *The Contemporary American Short Story Cycle: The Ethnic Resonance of Genre* (2001) and an editor of the *Portable American Realism and Naturalism Reader* (1997). In the excerpt below from the chapter entitled, "Narrative Methods: 'The Eyes of the World,'" Nagel characterizes Henry Fleming's fragmented and discrete experiences as the equivalent of the impressionistic school of artists who sought to capture the brief and ever-changing image of nature.]

The point of view Crane employed in *The Red Badge* is basically that of a limited third-person narrator whose access to data is restricted to the mind of the protagonist, Henry Fleming, to his sensory apprehensions and associated thoughts and feelings. In typical Impressionistic manner, Henry's experiences are discontinuous and fragmented and result in a novel composed of brief units. These scenes do not always relate directly to juxtaposed episodes, nor do they always develop the same themes. Furthermore, Henry's view of the battle is severely limited. He knows nothing of the strategy of the battle; he frequently cannot interpret the events around him because his information is obscured by darkness, smoke, or the noise of cannons; rumors spread quickly throughout his regiment, heightening the fear and anxiety of the men. Often, preoccupied by introspection, Henry's mind distorts the data it receives, transforming men into monsters and artillery shells into shrieking demons that leer at him. In short, Henry's view of things is limited, unreliable, and distorted, and yet a projection of the working of his mind becomes a dramatically realistic depiction of how war might appear to an ordinary private engaged in a battle in the American Civil War.

In an important sense, narrative method is the genius of *The Red Badge*. Of their own, the central events of the novel are commonplace. What gives the novel its unique quality is the method of its telling, its restriction of information. As Orm Øverland has pointed out,

> throughout *The Red Badge* (except in the first paragraph where, as it were, the "camera eye" settles down on the camp and the youth, and the concluding one where it again recedes) we in our imagined roles as spectators never have a larger view of the field than has the main character.

Many other Crane scholars have commented on this technique, and most of them invoke a visual metaphor, such as the "camera eye," to describe the method. Carl Van Doren, for example, wrote in the *American Mercury* in 1924 that Henry Fleming "is a lens through which a whole battle may be seen, a sensorium upon which all its details may be registered." Although Van Doren is overgenerous in his analysis of how much of the battle Henry actually sees, he is essentially correct in classifying the methodology of its rendition. Indeed, even thirty years after its initial publication, *The Red Badge* must have seemed most remarkable, for no third-person novel in American literature previously published had so severely limited its point of view. That such restriction is Impressionistic has been well established by Sergio Perosa:

> *The Red Badge of Courage* is indeed a triumph of impressionistic vision and impressionistic technique. Only a few episodes are described from the outside; Fleming's mind is seldom analyzed in an objective, omniscient way; very few incidents are extensively *told*. Practically every scene is filtered through Fleming's point of view and seen through his eyes. Everything is related to his *vision*, to his *sense*-perception of incidents and details, to his *sense*-reactions rather than to his psychological impulses, to his confused sensations and individual impressions.

There is somewhat more "telling" by the narrator than Perosa's comment suggests, and perhaps more interplay from Henry's "psychological impulses," but this formulation of the narrative method of the novel is essentially accurate. Although there are a few passages with an intrusive narrative presence, and a few other complicating devices involving temporal dislocations, the central device of the novel is the rendering of action and thought as they occur in Henry's mind, revealing not the whole of the battle, nor even the broad significance of it, but rather the meaning of this experience to him. The immediacy of the dramatic action is a product of the rendering of the sensory data of Henry's mind; the psychological penetration results from the mingling of experience with association, distortion, fantasy, and memory. A further implication of this method, one that is unsettling but realistic, is that the world presented to Henry is beyond his control, beyond even his comprehension. His primary relation to it is not so much a matter of his deeds as of his organization of sensation into language and pattern.

—James Nagel, "Narrative Methods: *The Eyes of the World.*" In *Stephen Crane and Literary Impressionism* (University Park: Pennsylvania State University Press, 1980): pp. 52–53.

DONALD PEASE ON HISTORY AND HEROIC ATTRIBUTES

[Donald Pease is the author of "Doing Justice to C. L. R. James's Mariners, Renegades and Castaways" (2000) and "After the Tocqueville Revival or, the Return of the Political" (1999). In the excerpt below from his article, "Fear, Rage, and the Mistrials of Representation in *The Red Badge of Courage,*" Pease discusses the absence of either historical or heroic attributes in Crane's narrative of a young Civil War soldier.]

In the April 1896 issue of *The Dial,* Army General A. C. McClurg, in a critical document interesting less for the general's insight into the novel than the direction of his criticism of it, bitterly denounced *The Red Badge of Courage* as a vicious satire of army life. "The hero of the book, if such he can be called, was an ignorant and stupid country lad without a spark of patriotic feeling or soldierly ambition," the general wrote. "He is throughout an idiot or a maniac and betrays no trace of the reasoning being. No thrill of patriotic devotion to cause or country ever moves his breast, and not even an emotion of manly courage." ⟨. . .⟩

Clearly Crane inflamed the general's ire by leaving political considerations out of his account altogether. Written at a time when the nation's historians were characterizing the political and ideological significance of seemingly every battle in the war, Crane's power derived from his decision to reverse the procedure. By stripping the names from the battles he describes, Crane releases the sheer force of the battle incidents unrelieved by their assimilation into a historical narrative frame. And like a naive social historian, General McClurg decided to make good on the debits in Crane's account. In his critical relation to the war novel he restored to the narrative what Crane carefully eliminated from Henry Fleming's confrontation with war: a political and moral frame of reference. ⟨. . .⟩

⟨. . .⟩ General McClurg in his review, then, did not wish to launch a personal attack on Private Fleming but to recover those representations Stephen Crane had withheld. As the general's review vividly attests, by 1896 these representations had become ingrained enough in the American character for one of her "representative men" to take their absence as a personal affront.

By mentioning General McClurg's reaction specifically, I do not mean to isolate its eccentricity, but to suggest that in its very force his reaction represents the urgent need to recover that sense of a developing American character Crane's account has taken leave of. Whether commentators attack this lack of character directly as General McClurg does in denouncing Private Fleming as a coward, or denounce it after a manner subtle enough to remain unconscious of it, as do more recent critics, by reading a coherent line of character development into the arbitrary incidents in Henry's life, the wish remains the same in both cases, to recover the sense of exemplary continuity, integrity, and significance for those Civil War events Stephen Crane has forcibly excised from official history. Crane acknowledges the urgency of this need by never failing to drive a wedge between the sheer contingency of Henry's battle experiences and those reflections on them that never account for so much as they displace these incidents with other concerns. What results is an ongoing sense of disorientation, a knowledge of Henry Fleming's involvement in a battle that history will later turn into a monumental event, but whose dimensions never presently convert into anything more than a series of discontinuous incidents, followed by pauses whose emptiness Henry can never fill with sufficient reflections.

—Donald Pease, "Fear, Rage, and the Mistrials of Representation in *The Red Badge of Courage*." In *American Realism: New Essays,* Eric J. Sundquist, ed. (Baltimore and London: The Johns Hopkins University Press, 1982): pp. 155–157.

DONALD PIZER ON THE AMBIGUITY OF HENRY FLEMING'S CHARACTER

[Donald Pizer is the author of "'Frank Norris' McTeague: Naturalism as Popular Myth" (2000) and "Bad Critical Writing" (1998). In the excerpt below from his article, "*The Red Badge of Courage*: Text, Theme, and Form," Pizer discusses the ambiguity of Henry Fleming's experience by pointing to the supernatural elements which work against traditional notions of a young man's "coming of age."]

The two opening paragraphs of *The Red Badge of Courage* constitute a paradigm for the themes and techniques of the novel as a whole. In its events and in much of its symbolism, the novel is a story of the coming of age of a young man through the initiatory experience of battle. But our principal confirmation of Henry's experiences as initiation myth is Henry himself, and Crane casts doubt—through his ironic narrative voice—on the truth and value of Henry's estimation of his adventures and himself. And so a vital ambiguity ensues.

The initiation structure of *The Red Badge* is evident both in the external action of the novel and in a good deal of the symbolism arising from event. A young untried soldier, wracked by doubts about his ability to perform well under fire, in fact does flee ignominiously during his first engagement. After a series of misadventures behind his own lines, including receiving a head wound accidentally from one of his own fellows, he returns to his unit, behaves estimably in combat, and receives the plaudits of his comrades and officers. On the level of external action, *The Red Badge is* thus a nineteenth-century development novel in compressed form. In such works, a young man (or woman) tries his mettle in a difficult world, at first believes himself weak and unworthy in the face of the enormous obstacles he encounters, but finally gains the experience necessary to cope with life and thus achieves as well a store of inner strength and conviction. Much of the symbolism in *The Red Badge* supports a reading of the work as developmental fiction, for one major pattern of symbolism in the novel rehearses the structure of the initiation myth. Henry is at first isolated by his childlike innocence. But after acquiring a symbol of group experience and acceptance (the red badge), he is guided by a supernatural mentor (the cheery soldier) through a night journey to reunion with his fellows; and in the next day's engagement he helps gain a symbolic token of passage into manhood (the enemy's flag).

But much in the novel also casts doubt on the validity of reading the work as an initiation allegory. Chief among these sources of doubt is Crane's ironic undermining at every turn of the quality of Henry's mental equipment and therefore of the possibility that he can indeed mature. Whenever Henry believes he has gained a significant height in his accomplishments and understanding, Crane reveals—by situational and verbal irony—how shallow a momentary resting place he has indeed reached. A typical example occurs after the enemy's first charge during the initial day of battle, when Henry grandiosely overestimates the character of a minor skirmish. ("So it was over at last! The supreme trial had been passed. The red, formidable difficulties of war had been vanquished.") This ironic deflation of Henry's self-evaluation continues unrelieved throughout the novel and includes as well Henry's final summing up, when, after in effect merely having survived the opening battle in the spring of a long campaign (with Gettysburg to follow!), he concludes that "the world was a world for him, though many discovered it to be made of oaths and walking sticks." ⟨. . .⟩

Crane also undermines the initiation structure of *The Red Badge* by including in the novel two major counterstructures. Initiation is essentially, a mythic statement of a faith in the potential for individual growth—that the forward movement of time is meaningful and productive because through experience we acquire both the

capacity to cope with experience and a useful knowledge of our-
selves and the world. But *The Red Badge* also contains two major
structures which imply that time is essentially meaningless, that all
in life is circular repetition, that only the superficial forms of the
repetition vary and thus are capable of being misunderstood as significant change and progress. 〈. . .〉

—Donald Pizer, "*The Red Badge of Courage:* Text, Theme, and Form,"
The South Atlantic Quarterly 84, no. 3 (Summer 1985): pp. 306–308.

KIRK M. REYNOLDS ON JAMES NAGEL'S READING OF HENRY FLEMING

[Kirk M. Reynolds is the author of "*The Red Badge of
Courage:* Private Henry's Mind as Sole Point of View." In the
excerpt below from his article, Reynolds disputes James
Nagel's reading of moral growth in Henry Fleming and
locates the real ambiguity of the novel in the fact that the
narrative voice is almost exclusively that of its young protagonist.]

Since its first publication in book form in 1895, Stephen Crane's *The
Red Badge of Courage,* now available in the authoritative edition by
Bradley and others, has elicited a spectrum of interpretations that
invariably are seeking a coherent structure that will adequately
account for the ending of the novel. When we read in the last paragraphs that Henry Fleming has become a man, "his soul changed,"
can we believe it? When we reach the last sentence of the novel,
whose observation about the appearance of sunshine on that rainy
day do we read? And what does such a final sentence indicate about
the meaning of the novel? The critics have argued inconclusively that
the ending is affirmative, ironic, ambiguous, or, because the problems seem irresolvable, that Crane's work is flawed. 〈. . .〉

James Nagel's recent study (1980) provides the most thorough
analysis of Crane's uses of the limited omniscient viewpoint—"the
natural expression of Literary Impressionism"—really a dual viewpoint that Nagel defines as follows:

The point of view Crane employed in *The Red Badge* is basically that of a limited third-person narrator whose access to data is restricted to the mind of the protagonist, Henry Fleming. . . . Although there are a few passages with an intrusive narrative presence, and a few other complicating devices involving temporal dislocations, the central device of the novel is the rendering of action and thought as they occur in Henry's mind, revealing not the whole of the battle, nor even the broad significance of it, but rather the meaning of this experience to him.

With this view of the narrator, Nagel points to Henry's "epiphany" in chapter 18, and, by finding that after Henry's epiphany "narrative irony ceases," he represents those critics who find the ending of the novel straightforward and indicative of moral growth in the young soldier. However, such a subtle narrative method as that described above by Nagel offers no clear explanation of just how one determines which sentences one will read as only accurate renderings of thoughts in Henry's mind and which sentences as including narrative commentary. ⟨. . .⟩

Because all previous interpretations, all of which suggest the dual viewpoint, fail to resolve the problems of the ending, I propose that, before we write off the work as flawed, we reevaluate Crane's novel as one in which the reader sees *only* through Henry's eyes and mind. There is not someone else watching. The novel merely seems to have an outside narrator until the subjective ending surprisingly redefine, the previous point of view to be only Henry's. The ending indicates not the novel's ambiguity but its point of view. *Red Badge* is an interior monologue. ⟨. . .⟩

To test this interpretation, we must see if the subjectivity of the last few paragraphs of *Red Badge* can redefine the point of view to be that of the boy Henry alone—an uncomfortable consideration for the reader. In such a case, upon reaching the novel's ending and supposing himself at comfortable objective distance, the reader, who has been amused watching the immature youth be victimized by dramatic irony, becomes also the victim of irony: he has been seduced into misreading the novel.

Let us look at the story before Crane's ending. Because many sentences throughout the novel include guide-verbs, such as "seemed," "thought," "felt," and "wished," that clearly indicate the subjective view of Henry, other passages that do not contain such guides must also be interpretable as purely subjective—or else the dual point of view exists.

The opening paragraph of the novel provides a combination of apparently objective details and subjective impressions:

> The cold passed reluctantly from the earth, and the retiring fogs revealed an army stretched out on the hills, resting. As the landscape changed from brown to green, the army awakened, and began to tremble with eagerness at the noise of rumors. It cast its eyes upon the roads, which were growing from long troughs of liquid mud to proper thoroughfares. A river, amber-tinted in the shadow of its banks, purled at the army's feet; and at night, when the stream had become of a sorrowful blackness, one could see across it the red, eyelike gleam of hostile camp-fires set in the low brows of distant hills. ⟨. . .⟩

—Kirk M. Reynolds, "*The Red Badge of Courage:* Private Henry's Mind as Sole Point of View," *South Atlantic Review* 52, no. 1 (January 1987): pp. 59–63.

BEN SATTERFIELD ON THE NOVEL AS HUMANISTIC WORK OF ART

[Ben Satterfield is the author of "Facing the Abyss: The Floating Opera and End of the Road" (1983) and "Multiculturalism, Miseducation and the New McCarthyism" (1992). In the excerpt below from his article "From Romance to Reality: The Accomplishment of Private Fleming," Satterfield reads *The Red Badge of Courage* as an affirmative and humanistic work of art and responds to those critics who argue for its religious significance.]

To offer yet another contribution to the interpretation of "so notoriously overanalyzed a novel" as *The Red Badge of Courage* is to invite the charge of performing a dispensable act. But just the opposite is true: a coherent and uncontradictory reading is necessary. This short novel by Stephen Crane has engendered critical and expository schisms of so profound a nature that there is not even common agreement as to what the book is about; in form, it is generally labeled a novel of initiation, a *Bildungsroman,* but in content, it has been called everything from a negative and dehumanized portrait of pessimistic-deterministic philosophy to an inspiring religious allegory. In fact, *The Red Badge,* while neither plotless nor obscure, remains something of an enigma on any level other than that of a war story, in spite of its having been pored over by myriad critics. My intention here is to present a tenable analysis that views the book as a consistent and unified work of art that is neither allegorical nor naturalistic, but essentially affirmative and humanistic in scope. ⟨. . .⟩

Since Crane relies so heavily upon it, imagery will be stressed as a key to meaning, with particular emphasis on animal imagery, the abundance of which makes it impossible to read the novel without being constantly aware of it. Although this imagery has been repeatedly cited, its dominance is not yet apparent to all. In the Stephen Crane issue of the *University of Minnesota Pamphlets on American Writers,* Jean Cazemajou's insistence is that "religious imagery prevails" in *The Red Badge of Courage.* Following this declaration, a few examples are quoted, including "the ghost of his flight," "column-like," and "the tattered man." These meager and dubious examples are then subsequently and inaccurately referred to as a "procession of religious images."

Most of the images in this novel are not religious in any recognizable sense; indeed, one would have to expand the definition of "religious" beyond credible limits to include "a specter of reproach" and "the creed of soldiers" as phrases appropriate to its meaning. The animal imagery, however, is not doubtful and permeates the novel. The first definite allusions occur in chapter one where the recruits are referred to as "prey" and "fresh fish," and the same type of imagery persists through the final chapter where one particular officer is described as a "whale"—an image that recalls the "fish" of chapter one. But despite the fact that over seventy comparisons of the men to animals have been counted in *The Red Badge of Courage* and one article has been written solely about animal imagery (in which is stated: "Excluding all the numerous sunken metaphors which imply animal-like action, this short novel contains at least 80 figures of speech employing animals or their characteristics"), this imagery has not been adequately explained nor its coherence demonstrated. The often noted (and I believe mistaken) interpretation of the animal imagery is that it reinforces Crane's "naturalism." ⟨. . .⟩

—Ben Satterfield, "From Romance to Reality: The Accomplishment of Private Fleming," *CLA Journal* 24, no. 4 (June 1981): pp. 451–453.

DANIEL SHANAHAN ON THE NATURE OF MARTIAL VIRTUE

[Daniel Shanahan is the author of "Affect and Cognition in Two Theories of the Origin of Language" (2000) and "We Are McWorld: The Globalization of Consumer Culture and Its Discontents" (1998). In the excerpt below from his article, "The Army Motif in *The Red Badge of Courage* as a Response to Industrial Capitalism," Shanahan discusses the nature of "martial virtue" in the novel with particular reference to a contemporary literary work, Edward Bellamy's *Looking Backward: 2000–1887*.]

Two of the more popularly successful attempts to draw on aspects of the "martial" experience of the Civil War as a way of addressing the social convulsion of a society hurtling into capitalism and industrialization did not actually portray the War itself, but both rely on an army motif to evoke the social climates of nascent competition and mechanization in the fictional worlds they create. Edward Bellamy's utopian *Looking Backward: 2000–1887* envisions a future society in which mechanization has been tamed and competition transformed into cooperation, largely through the aegis of a huge "industrial army" into which society, now harmonious and productive, has been organized. *Looking Backward* was the third most popular novel of its time, it produced a wave of nationalism in the country, and thus became a social event in its own right. ⟨. . .⟩

While there is no direct evidence that Stephen Crane read either Bellamy or Donnelly, it is hard to imagine that anyone who lived and traveled, as Crane did, in the literary circles of the 1890s could have avoided reading *Looking Backward*. ⟨. . .⟩

Crane wrote *The Red Badge of Courage* immediately after *Maggie: A Girl of the Streets,* a novel which presents a vision of contemporary society as a ruthlessly competitive domain in which all men—and women—are reduced to their predatory instincts and all of their distinguishing characteristics are effaced by the brutality to which they themselves become subject. The effects of emergent capitalism on American society are never far from view in *Maggie,* and given the novel's highly competitive social environment, it comes as no surprise that the theme of competition so thoroughly informs *Red Badge.* From the opening moments of the book, in which Crane portrays two soldiers arguing over rumors about troop movements, to the near-brawl that erupts before the first chapter closes—this time about how well the regiment will fight—contention is the dominant mode of social interaction. In the world Crane creates, the army is rife with internal contention even before it enters into the grand competition by which, Marx had argued only a few years before, industrial capitalism sustains itself.

But throughout the first half of the novel, the main character, Henry Fleming, is an exception to the rule of contention and competition as the dominant mode of behavior, and while it is common to see Henry as a character taken from romantic idealism about war to a tempered bravery, it is less common to see how Henry's reluctance to compete, and his later willingness to do so, punctuate his change in character.

Because he seems to lack the innate competitive instincts of the other men in the regiment, Henry never takes part in any of the arguing, sparring or contending that goes on between his fellows. In short, he fails to communicate with them on the terms in which they most frequently seem to communicate with one another, so he remains an outsider, and only nominally a member of the army. Only after he witnesses the death of his friend, Jim Conklin, does Henry begin to show signs of adopting the aggressiveness he will need to face the realities of war. ⟨. . .⟩

—Daniel Shanahan, "The Army Motif in *The Red Badge of Courage* as a Response to Industrial Capitalism," *Papers on Language & Literature* 32, no. 4 (Fall 1996): pp. 401–403.

[Michael Schneider is the author of "The Chattahoochee
River: A Linguistic Boundary" (1998) and "Bottom's
Dream, the Lion's Roar, and Hostility of Class Difference in
A Midsummer Night's Dream" (1987). In the excerpt below
from his article, "Monomyth Structure in *The Red Badge of
Courage*," Schneider discusses the novel in terms of
Northrop Frye's identification of the "quest-romance."]

As with many novels, it is the ending that has troubled many
readers of *The Red Badge of Courage*. Henry Binder's project, for
instance, which reconstructs the text from manuscript, is an effort,
in effect, to start over with a new novel free of the problem of the
ending. The problem is, as Mordecai Marcus puts it, "the apparent
discrepancy between the almost consistently instinctive motivation
of Henry Fleming and the concluding assertion that he has gained
a quiet but assertive manhood." Until the concluding paragraphs,
Crane's ironic touch shows Henry as a romantic, self-deluded
youth. When he imagines himself as a hero, he runs from the
enemy charge; then he reclaims his shattered self-esteem only
through the haphazard fortune of his "wound," from which the
novel takes its title. Reflecting on *Red Badge*'s pattern of accumu-
lating irony, C. C. Walcutt wrote that Crane "makes us see Henry
Fleming as an emotional puppet controlled by whatever sight he
sees at the moment," and if the book has a point it is that "Henry
has never been able to evaluate his conduct." ⟨. . .⟩

The problem of the ending is closely related to another issue of
Red Badge criticism; whether the novel should be regarded as a
realistic novel about the Civil War or whether it is a symbolic narrative about self-knowledge and psychological maturity. I will
show in this essay that *Red Badge* is close cousin to the archetypal
pattern of hero stories which Joseph Campbell has identified as the
hero monomyth and which Northrop Frye calls "quest-romance."
This pattern underlies *Red Badge* as a structural principle giving it
coherence and unity. Recognizing *Red Badge*'s kinship with this
pattern deepens its meaning without diminishing its realistic
power. The assertion at the end that Henry's soul has changed to
"quiet manhood" presents itself as a problem most sharply if we

regard the novel as exclusively realistic. Henry, at novel's end, is still a young man only three days removed from romantic books and embracing mother love. If, however, we regard Henry's adventure as quest-romance, the assertion of manhood attained is an expected concluding element of the formal structure. As Joseph Campbell says of the monomyth hero at the end of his adventure: "Having surpassed the delusions of his formerly self-assertive, self-defensive, self-concerned ego, he knows without and within the same repose."

There is much more than the ending of *Red Badge* that invites it to be read as quest-romance. The general outline of its action—departure from home and mother, entry into combat, and return—conforms to the nuclear unit of the monomyth identified by Campbell: separation, initiation, and return. Furthermore, Crane's lurid battle imagery, rife with monsters and serpents, encourages us to see an inner battle going on amid the outer battle. When Henry sees the enemy charge as "an onslaught of redoubtable dragons," for instance, the dragons are an image of Henry's fear, his inner enemy which must be confronted as part of growth into adulthood. Others have emphasized the symbolic aspect of *Red Badge,* and it is commonplace to observe that Henry's struggle with fear represents his own coming into manhood, the age-old story of a young man's initiation to life. Initiation ritual is closely linked with the dragon-killing of quest-romance. Indeed, this symbolic underpinning to the *Red Badge* would, perhaps, require no elaboration but for the question of the ending—the seeming disjunction between the straightforward assertion of growth and the ironic undercutting which precedes it—and the resistance among many critics to a symbolic reading of this novel. The symbolic reading, however, is especially important to the *Red Badge* because it allows a way to resolve Crane's irony with his shift in tone at the end. ⟨. . .⟩

—Michael Schneider, "Monomyth Structure in *The Red Badge of Courage," American Literary Realism 1870–1910,* 20, no. 1 (Fall 1987): pp. 45–46.

ROBERT SHULMAN ON TRAUMA IN CRANE'S MYTH OF
THE CIVIL WAR

[Robert Shulman is the author of "Sokal's Hoax: The Sham
that Shook the Academy" (2000) and "Dashiell Hammett's
Social Vision" (1985). In the excerpt below from his article,
"*The Red Badge* and Social Violence: Crane's Myth of His
America," Shulman discusses Crane's use of specific images
and narrative ruptures to thematize the trauma of his myth
of the Civil War.]

The Red Badge of Courage is Crane's response to the underlying
violence, turmoil and savagery of post-Civil War America. Crane,
however, has still not received enough credit for conveying through
the war world of his novel the inner meaning of the social, political, racial and economic realities he transformed into the myth of
war in *The Red Badge.* By "the myth of war" I mean the timeless,
larger-than-life, suggestive quality that emerges from Crane's dominant imagery of war and fog, from his disorienting irony and
failure to provide clear connectives, from his sense of anarchic
breakdown and uncertainty, and from the savage violence, shifting
shapes, and diminished, groping protagonist that together give *The
Red Badge* its distinguishing energy. This configuration constitutes
a "myth" in the sense that it embodies a dominant imagery and set
of emotionally charged attitudes that express the meaning of life
not only for the author but also for a significant number of others
in his culture. ⟨. . .⟩

⟨. . .⟩ The Civil War setting, for example, is an embarrassment.
But unlike Tolstoy in *War and Peace,* Zola in *The Debacle,* or
Stendhal in the battle scenes of *The Charterhouse of Parma,* Crane
is not primarily interested in rendering with circumstantial
realism a period thirty years in the past. His primary commitment
is to render the psychology of battle, especially the inner rhythms
of perception, fear and fantasy; to test inadequate views of
heroism, identity and human nature; to probe the modern epistemological situation; and to establish for himself what will suffice.
Although he researched Chancellorsville, *The Battles and Leaders
of the Civil War,* and looked at Brady's photographs, instead of a
complex rendering of the Civil War in particular, Crane is mainly
interested in the testing of a young American Everyman—in the

timeless, universal drama of a young man confronting the existential facts of death and fear, and the perhaps more time-bound drama of perceptions often beautifully warped by emotion and self-interest in a fog-shrouded inner and outer world where knowledge is shifting and uncertain. One result of this emphasis on the inner drama, on the flow of perceptions and feelings, and the relative neglect of sustained, external social specification is a novel that moves through metaphors toward universals. We recall the boy, the battle, the forest, the fog, the fear, the attack and retreat, the waiting, the flag, the sun. ⟨. . .⟩ Crane's book, then, is indebted to fictional conventions rooted in Pilgrim's journey through a troubled world and in the transformed imagery and techniques of his own Methodist tradition. ⟨. . .⟩

In America the sense of violent conflict and anarchic breakdown that animates *The Red Badge* reached a climax during the strike-ridden, depression years 1892–94 when Crane was conceiving and writing his novel. But these were not the first war-like years of Crane's lifetime. ⟨. . .⟩ For Stephen Crane, the violent events of 1877 are prime candidates. Crane was six, and in a minister's family in New Jersey the talk could not have avoided the burning and killing from Pittsburgh to San Francisco, the battles between Federal troops and urban crowds as close by as Maryland and Pennsylvania, the railroads shut down across the country and a spontaneous general strike broken with troops and bloodshed; in the nearby coal mining country, more strikes, the devastation of poverty, and the recent violence of the Molly Maguires (Crane's uncle lived in Molly Maguire country)—all this the culmination of four years of economic depression, wage cutbacks, and watered stock, with the specter of anarchism or communism seriously invoked, along with the troops, who had to be recalled from their assaults on the Sioux to take care of uprisings closer to home.

—Robert Shulman, "*The Red Badge* and Social Violence: Crane's Myth of His America," *The Canadian Review of American Studies* 12, no. 1 (Spring 1981): pp. 1–2, 4.

Henry Binder on the *Red Badge of Courage* Nobody Knows

[Henry Binder is the editor of *The Red Badge of Courage: An Episode of the American Civil War* (1982) and "Donald Pizer, Ripley Hitchcock and *The Red Badge of Courage*" (1979). In the excerpt below from his article, "*The Red Badge of Courage* Nobody Knows," Binder discusses a very different version of the novel which exists only in manuscript form and a version for which Binder makes a case for a highly ironic reading of Henry Fleming.]

This essay celebrates an unknown novel by Stephen Crane entitled *The Red Badge of Courage,* a novel that only a few of Crane's friends and early editors ever had a chance to read, a *Red Badge of Courage* that existed only in Crane's manuscript, not in any published version of the story. In the manuscript, the novel is longer and much different from the *Red Badge* that was first issued as a book by D. Appleton & Co. of New York in October, 1895. The Appleton edition pleased the contemporary audience and has become a classic of American literature, but it is not what Crane conceived the story to be. Most contemporary readers found the Appleton *Red Badge* to be an account of a young man's growth from confused youth to resolute manhood; but ever since the first close readings appeared in the 1940s, modern critics have argued inconclusively as to whether or not this growth takes place; and still others have said that *Red Badge* is a flawed work which cannot be satisfactorily explicated. What happened is that Crane wrote an ironic story in the manuscript, a story in which the central character does not undergo any positive growth; and then apparently in response to editorial suggestions at Appleton, made or allowed two series of deletions in the novel just prior to publication. These deletions confused the original irony; reduced the psychological complexity of Henry Fleming, the main character; also obscured the function of Wilson and the tattered man; and left the text incoherent at several places, in particular the final chapter. The critical disagreements about *Red Badge* arise mainly because of the problematic state of the text Appleton published, a text which, owing to the cuts, no longer embodied Crane's intentions. ⟨. . .⟩

In the deleted conclusion to chapter seven, seeing that nature's laws will not justify his flight, Henry decides that nature is universally malevolent. Repeating this thought in an angrier mood at the close of chapter ten, he concludes that nature must have created glory in order to entice men to war "because ordinary processes could not furnish deaths enough." The original chapter twelve presents a climax in this philosophizing, with Henry envisioning himself the "growing prophet of a world-reconstruction," the spiritual founder of a "new world modelled by the pain of his life," prepared to show men the folly of their tradition-founded illusions. All of these monologues are empty rationalizations which Henry later refers to as his "rebellions." His strategy in rebelling is to envision his behavior as determined by a universal causality and then assume a vain stance of contempt for the race of human beings who, unlike him, are unable to recognize the deterministic state of affairs he sees. At the close of the original chapter fifteen, Henry has returned to his regiment and feels relatively secure that he will not be discovered as a coward, but when he learns from Wilson that other men were separated from the regiment he is angered that the previous day's "experiences" which occasioned his rebellions are no proof of his uniqueness among men; he retrospectively feels a contempt for "all his grapplings and tuggings with fate and the universe." ⟨. . .⟩

Most of the second-stage deletions were made in chapter sixteen and in chapter twenty-five (the final chapter in the original numbering before chapter twelve was removed). In Crane's plotting of the original *Red Badge,* these two chapters contained markedly parallel material that provided an ironic frame for Henry Fleming's combat successes in the intervening chapters, seventeen through twenty-four. The cuts made in these chapters can be seen as of a piece with the first-stage excisions in that references to Henry's earlier and already deleted rebellions against nature were removed, and, again, interior monologues in which he explained his behavior and his "fate" as cosmically decided were cut. Also deleted was material that specifically laid bare Henry's enduring meanness and vanity.

—Henry Binder, "*The Red Badge of Courage* Nobody Knows," *Studies in the Novel* 10, no. 1 (Spring 1978): pp. 9, 12–13.

CAROL B. HAFER ON IRONY IN *THE RED BADGE OF COURAGE*

[Carol B. Hafer is the author of "The Red Badge of Absurdity: Irony in *The Red Badge of Courage*." In the excerpt below from that article, Hafer discusses Henry Fleming as an anti-hero, arguing against those critics who read his characterization as a young man achieving self-knowledge and manhood.]

Most critics of *The Red Badge of Courage* see the novel as tracing the development of Henry Fleming from youth to manhood or from raw recruit to seasoned soldier. These critics excuse Henry's desertion on the first day of battle and his lying about the wound he has received on the ground that these actions are normal and lead to Henry's attainment of self-knowledge and manhood on the second day of battle. On the other hand, critics who discern no change in Henry during the second day interpret his desertion as the normal reaction of one under fire for the first time and find it of value to Henry in providing him with the experience which leads to his acquiring control over his fear on the second day, not as resulting in his attaining self-knowledge or manhood. ⟨. . .⟩

In the first place, the title *The Red Badge of Courage* is itself ironic; for the badge that Henry receives is a badge of shame or absurdity, rather than a badge of courage. Henry's badge is a blow on the head given him by one of his own comrades when Henry blocks his retreat in an attempt to obtain the latest news about the progress of battle, not a bullet sustained in combat against the enemy. Furthermore, had Henry remained fighting with his regiment instead of deserting, he would have known the outcome of the battle and would have had no need to block the retreating soldier to obtain the news.

Second, while several critics praise Henry's courage on the second day of battle, they fail to point out that Henry only stands and fights when he is "out of it." Throughout the novel, Henry in combat is described in terms of sleep, unconsciousness, and insanity. For example, Henry awakens and finds himself a knight; in combat, he finds himself "unconsciously in advance"; and when he charges, he runs "like a madman . . . his eyes almost closed, and the scene . . . a wild blur." ⟨. . .⟩

Third, it is ironic that Henry at the end of the second day remains egocentric and subject to delusions—in spite of his so-called rejection of his earlier gospels and his assertion that he is a man. While Henry does arrive at an assessment of himself (Chapter XXIV) it is—like his assessment of himself in Chapter XV—based upon unrealistic assumptions and/or upon a vainglorious view of his accomplishments. At the end of the second day of battle, for example, Henry interprets his part in the events of the last two days as follows:

> Regarding his procession of memory he felt gleeful and unregretting, for in it his public deeds were paraded in great and shining prominence. Those performances which had been witnessed by his fellows marched now in wide purple and gold having various deflections.

Although Henry does feel haunted by his flight of the day before, it is only "for a moment." Furthermore, when he recalls his desertion of the "tattered" soldier, it is only "for an instant" that he feels a chilling sweat come over him—a sweat at the thought of being discovered, rather than a sweat of remorse for his action and of pity for the seriously wounded man.

—Carol B. Hafer, "The Red Badge of Absurdity: Irony in *The Red Badge of Courage*," *CLA Journal* 14, no. 4 (June 1971): pp. 440–442.

Jean Cazemajou on the "Religion of Peace" and the War Archetype

[Jean Cazemajou is the author of "Les Metamorphoses du moi dans l'autobiographie d'Annie Dillard, an *American Childhood*" (1995) and "Mediators and Mediation in Rudolfo Anaya's Trilogy: *Bless Me, Ultima, Heart of Atzlan* and *Tortuga*" (1988). In the excerpt below from his article "*The Red Badge of Courage:* The "Religion of Peace" and the War Archetype," Cazemajou discusses such mythic elements as the rebirth of Nature which work against any reading of a fully individualized character.]

Any examination of Stephen Crane's mental processes ought to begin by referring to his "irony of soul," a term he himself used in "This Majestic Lie," a story in *Wounds in the Rain*. He rejected one-sided views on human problems, for even if his dominant voice was one of dissent, he never fell into the trap of nihilistic icono-clasm. Irony often serves as a vehicle for a veiled but deeply-felt sense of justice; Crane's irony is of that kind. What he seems to strive for in his work is the projection of a mental image to convey his personal conception of truth. Moving as he does in the sphere of abstractions and unresolved polarities, he often reduces his characters to a single feature in order to sketch their psychological progress along allegorical lines. This mythic approach to reality is a constant in his work: such primordial ideas as Mother, Child, Sin, Rebirth, War, and Peace operate in his writings as archetypal antagonists which evoke a dialectical tension. One consequence of this semantic structure is that in his writings no process of individualization is ever sufficiently complete to fill out the image of any character, even in Crane's most deeply wrought character studies. His artistic orientation precluded a sense of obligation to make his pictures picturesque or his characters thoroughly defined. That is one element of his comment on the genesis of *The Red Badge of Courage:* "It was essential that I should make my battle a type and name no names. . . ." ⟨. . .⟩

The descriptive force of Crane's style may lead one to read that novel as if it were an introduction to the sound and fury of real combat. Specific details of camp life, preparations for attacks, charges and countercharges, captures of prisoners, and seizures of enemy flags serve to convey the illusion of verisimilitude. Indeed, these details sufficiently parallel reality to allow one scholar to argue convincingly that Crane had the Battle of Chancellorsville in mind when he wrote *The Red Badge of Courage*. But the picture of battle given in the novel is blurred and limited in scope. It is not "war," but only war seen through the eyes of one raw recruit, a "youth." For him battle is chaos and confusion.

That is, however, only one possible view of war. The novel balances it with another, in which a world at peace continually intrudes on the smoke and destruction. Again, it is through the eyes of the youth that this antidote to war is visualized. He associates peace with images of rural harmony. Simultaneously frightened and fascinated by violence, Henry displays ambivalent tendencies. Tired of the routine of farm life, he is a dreamer soon carried away by the war hysteria that sweeps the land and reaches him first through the sound of a church bell ringing "the twisted news of a great battle." It makes him decide to escape from the monotony of chores by plunging into adventure. Soon after enlisting, however, he decides that endless drilling in camp is no better than "endless rounds from the house to the barn." And as the story unfolds a small number of flashbacks evoke the memory of peace, sharp and bright against the blurred image of battle: the warm farewell scenes of chapter 1, the crisp, gay circus parade of chapter 5, the cosy family meals and cool swimming parties of chapter 12—all introduce a universe in which everything is familiar and where a refreshing harmony of man with Nature prevails. These vignettes remind us of Whitman's glorification of life and the rebirth of Nature in his notes on the same battle.

—Jean Cazemajou, "*The Red Badge of Courage:* The 'Religion of Peace' and the War Archetype." In *Stepen Crane in Transition: Centenary Essays,* Joseph Katz ed. (Dekalb: Northern Illinois University Press, 1972): pp. 54–57.

N. E. Dunn on the Common Man's *Iliad*

[N. E. Dunn is the author of "Riddling Leaves: Robinson's 'Luke Havergal'" (1972) and "The Significance of Upward Mobility in *Martin Eden*" (1972). In the excerpt below from the article, "The Common Man's *Iliad*," Dunn discusses the novel in terms of a type of allegory with analogues to Homer's great war epic, the *Iliad*.]

In *American Literary Scholarship* the long critical debate over ironic intent in *The Red Badge of Courage* was reported to be resolved by the late seventies. Critical commentary of the 1980s, however, reveals that the complexities inherent in Crane's novelette continue to elicit disparate interpretations. For example, although much recent scholarship has seen the novel as satirical exposé of the title character, James Nagel, in his 1980 study of Crane's work, reverts to the older view of *The Red Badge* as *Bildungsroman*. ⟨. . .⟩

Now that current literary theory is willing to entertain the concept of intertextual relationships perhaps it will become more hospitable to literary allegory, long neglected in relation to modern literature as Edwin Honig noted in *Dark Conceit: The Making of Allegory.* Whether or not the term itself is used, modern hermeneutics, in its current interpretive efforts with "the veil of words," to use Gerald L. Bruns's recurrent phrase, is engaged in the recognition and interpretation of the allegorical mode in numerous modern texts. ⟨. . .⟩

On one level, in *The Red Badge* Crane is giving an old tale its second telling. His is not the complex allegorical mode described by Brun, however, which emphasizes a general theological frame of reference, but the relatively simple device of sustaining parallels with an earlier literary work to help him say efficiently what he has to say. Hence the emphasis here on "literary" allegory. The fact that the older literature remains pertinent to the later writer's thinking indicates that both are dealing with archetypal matter. Thus the author can write economically by reminding the reader of the earlier dramatization of the universal problem at hand while retaining the liberty to make his own commentary on the subject and at the same time provide a test for the validity of interpretation within his own text.

Whether war is the subject of the novel or one of its subjects or one of the methods of dramatizing commentary on larger subjects, *The Red Badge of Courage* is a war story, and one of the ways in which Crane clarifies and intensifies his own commentary is to capitalize on the most dramatic war story of them all, the *Iliad.* That Crane worked in the heroic tradition has been noted, in a general sense; the point here is not to review proof that he did so, but to explore specific parallels between *The Red Badge* and its specific frame of reference in order to see what those parallels helped Crane to say on his subject, in the text as he allowed it to be published.

Some of the Homeric elements in the novel are self-evident. Telling details include Crane's adaptation of the stock epithet, for example—"the loud soldier," "the tall soldier," "the youth"—and passages of verbatim repetition, characteristic of the ancient epic. Less conclusive but highly suggestive are occasional poetic passages full of the trochees, dactyls and spondees of heroic verse, such as the close of Chapter VII and the opening of Chapter VIII. Not to be disregarded, however, is the fact that Crane uses the central character, early in the novel, to invite comparison between his war story and the epic war story. Henry makes overtly Homeric references in his own thinking, as in his early daydreams about the nature of heroism in the ancient Greek epics and his famous lament that his mother did not tell him to return from the war "with his shield or on it." Occasionally Crane's very phrasing is also overtly Homeric, as in Chapter XXII, where Henry views portions of "the hard fight" and "the pitiless monotony of conflicts." Stentor's "voice of triple brass" finds its ironical application in Crane's "Stentorian speeches of the artillery"—another direct allusion from deep within the story, part of the continuing network of clues indicating that Crane had in mind, and wished the reader to keep in mind, the Homeric epic as background pointing up the satirical absurdity of situation in *The Red Badge.*

—N. E. Dunn, "The Common Man's *Iliad*," *Comparative Literature Studies* 21, no. 3 (Fall 1984): pp. 270–272.

BILL BROWN ON THE WAR GAME

[Bill Brown is the author of "The Secret Life of Things (Virginia Woolf and the Matter of Modernism)" (1999) and "How to Do Things with Things (A Toy Story)" (1998). In the excerpt below from his chapter entitled "The War Game: Bodies in Motion, Bodies at Rest," Brown discusses the significance of spectator sports in 1890's America as a metaphor for the Civil War and its pictorial representation.]

While Crane consciously tells the story of a youth's initiation in battle, his text unconsciously begins to tell an altogether different story: it exhibits a cultural dynamic whereby the mass circulation of the image of the American male as athlete suppresses the central residue of war, the corpse, and helps to efface a prior corporeal archive, the photographs of the Civil War dead. The degree to which this archive seems to resurface in *The Red Badge of Courage* is the degree to which the novel rewrites the problematic of impressionism as a question about the impressions of the camera, just as it rewrites the problematic of realism as a question about the production, circulation, and manipulation of *real images.* Fully agreeing with the argument that Crane seeks "to reinterpret the war through the cultural lenses" of the nineteenth century, I want to think through these very metaphorics of vision, which Crane criticism irresistibly deploys, to confront the way his war fiction reinterprets the war—and materializes the war—through the cultural lens of the lens itself. Within the image culture established foremost by the amusement industries, the question of "reality" gives way to a question about whether the image will incite private fixation or instill public enthusiasm, a question about how the image will be instrumentalized for ends other than amusement. 〈. . .〉

Amused by the certainty with which reviewers of his novel believed its author to be a veteran, Crane explained to John Hilliard that, though he had "never smelled even the powder of a sham battle," he got his "sense of the rage of conflict on the football field." If, then, the football imagery simply records this biographical fact, it also participates in the specular metaphorization that took hold in the 1890s, where football and war all but inevitably appear as simulacra of each other. Combat imagery pervades the newspaper reports of football games, including Crane's own. And by the time some of the nation's most famous athletes volunteered to fight in the war against Spain, Richard Harding Davis, the country's foremost sportswriter and most famous war correspondent, could say of the celebrated assault on San Juan Hill that the soldiers fought with "the same spirit that once sent these men down a white-washed field against their opponents' rush-line."

—Bill Brown, "The War Game: Bodies in Motion, Bodies at Rest." In *The Material Unconscious: American Amusement, Stephen Crane & the Economies of Play* (Cambridge, Mass. and London: Harvard University Press, 1996): pp. 125–127.

JAMES M. COX ON THE PURITY OF WAR

[James M. Cox is the author of "Henry Adams: The Letters and the Life" (1991) and "Tom Sawyer: Performer and Chief Entertainer" (1999). In the excerpt below from his article, "*The Red Badge of Courage:* The Purity of War," Cox discusses the novel as a superlative fiction of the Civil War by pointing out many of the details which Crane omits and which the reader has traditionally come to expect.]

Being both civilized and instinctual, both science and art, war is at once dynamic and inertial. It carries with it all the acceleration at the command of civilization to discover new and more powerful forms of weaponry just as it forever retains the possibility of hand-to-hand combat. The very word "arms" evokes the development from club through gun-powder to rifle to bomb at the same time that it refers to the aggressive upper limbs of the body. The combination of acceleration and inertia works through the emotions attending war. War is after all a hastening toward death; it is for the young, who, whether eager for it or forced into it, whether reckless or afraid, whether angry or appalled, find themselves both rushing and rushed toward an end that by the logic of peace ought to be further in their future. ⟨. . .⟩

All of which brings us to the Civil War—the one war that, for all its horror, has come down to us as a just war. ⟨. . .⟩ There were the day-to-day accounts in hundreds of newspapers, there were the letters home; then came the endless postwar accounts by participants, the 128 volumes of Official Records published by the United States Government, the countless histories of the war that continue to be written, and finally the innumerable fictive efforts to capture the "reality" of the war. ⟨. . .⟩

To see, in what we never doubt is a Civil War novel, just how little there is of what we traditionally associate with the historical Civil War, may not tell us what the novel is, but will at least impress us with what it is not. Not only are there no actual place names; there are no fictive place names. If there is topography in the form of a small river or an open field or a forest, it remains utterly generalized. There is exactly one mention of Richmond and Washington. There is no Grant or Lee or Hooker or Jackson or Meade or A. P. Hill. There is not even a North or a South. Even the terms "Yankee" and "Rebel" appear only once or twice as "yank" and "reb." There is no fight for the union or against slavery. There is not a mention of Abraham Lincoln or Jefferson Davis. ⟨. . .⟩ Finally, there is no romance in the book—no real girl left behind or met—no letters from home, no sense of a society behind or outside the society of the battlefield. True there is Henry's mother and a girl schoolmate Henry believes is looking at him as he readies for departure (this all stated in a few paragraphs in the first chapter), but they are left behind as completely as Aunt Charity in *Moby Dick* when the *Pequod* makes its plunge into the lone Atlantic.

To see what is left out—or better, cut away—is to see how Crane achieved both reduction and concentration of his vision to the field of battle and to the single consciousness of a private soldier. He emerged with an incredibly short novel—shorter even than *The Scarlet Letter*—whose twenty-four short chapters stand at once as reminders of the twenty-four books of *The Iliad* and as a line of sentinels marking the violently abrupt sequence of war. The very first paragraph of the book sets the scene:

> The cold passed reluctantly from the earth, and the retiring fogs revealed an army stretched out on the hills, resting. As the landscape changed from brown to green, the army awakened, and began to tremble with eagerness at the noise of rumors. It cast its eyes upon the roads, which were growing from long troughs of liquid mud to proper thoroughfares. A river, amber-tinted in the shadow of its banks, purled at the army's feet; and at night, when the stream had become of a sorrowful blackness, one could see across it the red, eyelike gleam of hostile campfires set in the low brows of distant hills.

So much is done here. First there is the pathetic fallacy hard at work throughout the passage: the cold *reluctantly* passing, the fogs *retiring,* the river *purling* by day and *sorrowful* at night. Nature itself is being personified as if it had a human will, and at the end of the paragraph it has become an animated form containing the eyelike gleam of hostile campfires set in the *brows* of distant hills. Even more important, the natural process reveals the army stretched out and resting, awakening, and trembling at the noise of rumors. ⟨. . .⟩

—James M. Cox, "*The Red Badge of Courage:* The Purity of War," *Southern Humanities Review* 25, no. 3 (Summer 1991): pp. 306–309.

HAROLD BEAVER ON THE HERO AS VICTIM

[Harold Beaver is the author of "Mardi: A Sum of Inconsistencies" (1984) and "Herman Melville: Prophetic Mariner" (1983). In the excerpt below from his article, "Stephen Crane: The Hero as Victim," Beaver discusses the heroic idea in late nineteenth-century America.]

> We picture the world as thick with conquering and elate
> humanity, but here, with the bugles of the tempest pealing,
> it was hard to imagine a peopled earth. One viewed the
> existence of man then as a marvel, and conceded a glamor
> of wonder to these lice, which were caused to cling to a
> whirling, fire-smote, ice-locked, disease-stricken, space-
> lost bulb. The conceit of man was explained by this storm
> to be the very engine of life. (*The Blue Hotel,* Chapter 8)

By the late nineteenth century the heroic ideal, though noisily encouraged in romantic fiction and by the popular press, had become harder and harder to sustain. For the myth of heroism was dependent on free will. But what Mendel and Ricardo and Marx and Darwin and Freud and Malthus had seemingly taught was that man was trapped; that he was the unsuspecting victim of genetic and economic and political and evolutionary and psychological forces, including an ever-spiralling population growth. The myth of heroism, moreover, depended on a vision of an integrated society with its own economic and sexual hierarchies, its own natural and supernatural controls. But, by the end of the century, the whole universe, it seemed, had disintegrated into a chaos of competing and anarchic forces receding ever faster to a state of entropic collapse. Such forces, by definition, were beyond human control. No counter-attack, however defiant, could be waged by an individual alone. ⟨. . .⟩

Stephen Crane was among the most self-conscious of this new breed of heroic writers. Henry Adams, his fellow American, chose to confront the *intellectual* responsibility of opting for anarchy. Crane chose to confront the *moral* responsibility (amid 'the bugles of the tempest pealing') of reeling through the blizzard. For it was as if a blizzard had struck the old American certainties. The new forces of Hegelian idealism and Darwinian biology and economic determinism—of evolution, class warfare, and heredity—were peculiarly stacked against the old Jeffersonian belief in personal self-control. Romantic individualism quickly soured, in the decades after the Civil War, to a documentary pessimism. Even before 1860 a brilliant minority of American writers, which included Hawthorne and Melville, had opted for pessimism. But now there were mass deserters. By 1900 the cleft between high art and 'pop' art was complete. It opened a chasm between serious fiction and fun, or escapist uplift, in westerns and athletic 'profiles' of which we are the inevitable heirs. For it was in this generation that the moral rewards of capitalism were first subverted; that Horatio Alger's call of 'rags to riches', 'Log Cabin to White House', was finally undercut by the new Naturalist Novel. The hero of self-improvement, U.S.-style, was shown, for good or ill, to be a mere victim of circumstances and/or his own illusions.

One native response was to ask: 'So what?' 'What, in short', in the words of William James, 'is the truth's cash value in experiential terms?'. But pragmatism was of little use to men who felt already doomed; for whom both Christianity and the promise of the Greek Revival had failed; who felt excluded from both the old religious and the Homeric appeals to personal glory. Like Dante, the young Stephen Crane awoke to find all confused, all lost. 'He had long despaired of witnessing a Greeklike struggle.' He aimed to fight his way out of that modern *selva oscura,* or Darwinian jungle. *The Red Badge of Courage* was to be his report from the jungle.

It appeared in 1895, a year after Kipling's *The Jungle Book,* four years before Conrad's *Heart of Darkness.* Crane was still only twenty-four years old. His subject was that of the hunters and the hunted, of the predators and the victims (much as that of Joel Chandler Harris's *Uncle Remus* tales) in a savagely destructive world. But his literary talent lay far from vernacular or folk tale. It comprised, above all, a split-second marksmanship in stalking his prey, nicknamed by contemporary photojournalists the 'snapshot'. This new heroic style was to rival Homer's for clarity. ⟨. . .⟩

—Harold Beaver, "Stephen Crane: The Hero as Victim," *The Yearbook of English Studies* 12 (1982): pp. 186–187.

ALFRED HABEGGER ON CRANE'S REPRESENTATION OF SPEECH

[Alfred Habegger is the author of *The Father: A Life of Henry James, Sr.* (1994) and *Gender, Fantasy and Realism in American Literature: The Rise of American Literary Realism in W. D. Howells and Henry James* (1982). In the excerpt below from his article, "Fighting Words: The Talk of Men at War in *The Red Badge*," Habegger discusses the historical relevance of the soldiers' *spoken* language from the perspective of the 1890's America.]

In discussing Crane's representation of speech, I will not be concerned with talk that is metaphorical rather than literal—"the courageous words of the artillery and the spiteful sentences of the musketry." Neither will I have much to say about the many passages in which Henry Fleming's unarticulated thoughts are rendered in language and imagery he himself would not have used. "Minds, he said, were not made all with one stamp and colored green." "He had been out among the dragons, he said." The diction, the absence of quotation marks, and the familiarity of the narrative convention these sentences follow all announce that "said" is not to be taken literally. (Obvious as the convention may be, Crane himself called attention to it in one sentence: "But [Henry] said, *in substance*, to himself that if the earth and the moon were about to clash, many persons would doubtless plan to get upon roofs to witness the collision" [italics mine].) I am confining my attention here only to those passages that represent *spoken* language, whether that language is recorded in direct discourse or summarized by Crane in what is traditionally called indirect discourse.

Although I will also ignore the much-discussed problem of "dialect," taking this term to refer to the presentation of regional or uncultivated speech through nonstandard orthography, it will be necessary to comment briefly on the generalized countrified traditionalism of the soldiers' talk. Some of their statements—"Well, I swan," "I'm a gone coon," "Be keerful, honey, you'll be a-ketchin' flies"—surely had an old-timey feel for Crane's first readers. Perhaps the same was true for "kit-an'-boodle," "jim-hickey," "chin-music," "skedaddle," "fresh fish," "fight like hell-roosters," "smart as a steel trap." Most of the mild oaths and curses probably had an old-fashioned flavor by 1895—"make way, dickens [i.e., devil] take it all," "by ginger" [i.e., Jesus], "Great Jerusalem." The fact that Crane was able to introduce undisguised profanity into the next-to-last charge—"Where in hell yeh goin'?" and "Gawd damn their souls"—tell us that the various euphemistic oaths were not simply an evasive concession to public taste. They also contribute to the picture of life in the 1860s as seen from the 1890s.

The character with the strongest rural twang is the tattered man, whose speech—"a reg'lar jim-dandy," "there's a bat'try comin' helitywhoop," "first thing that feller knowed he was dead"—shows none of Henry's anxiety at being taken for a greenhorn. Even so, humor and irony are well within the tattered man's range:

> "Oh, I'm not goin' t' die yit. There too much dependin' on me fer me t' die yit. No, sir! Nary die! I *can't!* Ye'd oughta see th' swad a' chil'ren I've got, an' all like that."
>
> The youth glancing at his companion could see by the shadow of a smile that he was making some kind of fun. ⟨...⟩

⟨...⟩ Framed by Crane's terse, up-to-date, and highly individualized prose, these and other locutions and speeches helped give the soldiers' talk a slightly quaint, historical feel. The novel had an overwhelming impact not because it revived the history of battles and leaders and official political rhetoric, but because it achieved an effect analogous to that of the new social history of our own time, which tries to revive the unofficial voices, the unexpressed experiences. Of course, Crane was chiefly interested (in this respect also, perhaps, resembling some of our own historians) in generating an *illusion* of factual excavation and reconstitution. It was the glaring disparities between his language as narrator and that of his characters that helped turn his trick.

—Alfred Habegger, "Fighting Words: The Talk of Men at War in *The Red Badge*," *Critical Essays on Stephen Crane's "The Red Badge of Courage,"* ed. Donald Pizer (Boston: G. K. Hall & Co., 1990): pp. 231–232.

Works by
Stephen Crane

Maggie, A Girl of the Streets. (1893).

The Red Badge of Courage. (1895).

George's Mother. (1896).

The Third Violet. (1897).

Active Service. (1899).

The O'Ruddy (with Robert Barr). (1903).

Works About
Stephen Crane

Bais, H. S. S. *Stephen Crane: Pioneer in Technique*. New Delhi: Crown Publications, 1988.

Beer, Thomas. *Stephen Crane: A Study in American Letters*. New York: A. A. Knopf, 1923.

Benfey, Christopher. *The Double Life of Stephen Crane*. New York: Alfred A. Knopf, 1992.

Bergon, Frank. *Stephen Crane's Artistry*. New York: Columbia University Press, 1975.

Berryman, John. *Stephen Crane: A Critical Biography*. New York: Farrar, Straus & Giroux, 1950.

Binder, Henry. "Donald Pizer, Ripley Hitchcock, and *The Red Badge of Courage*." *Studies in the Novel* 11, no. 2 (Summer 1979): 216–23.

Bloom, Harold, ed. *Modern Critical Interpretations of Stephen Crane's* The Red Badge of Courage. Broomall, Pennsylvania: Chelsea House Publishers (1987).

Bowers, Fredson, ed. *The Works of Stephen Crane*. 10 vols. Charlottesville: University Press of Virginia, 1969–76.

Cady, Edwin Harrison. *Stephen Crane*. Boston: Twayne Publishers, 1980.

Cazemajou, Jean. *Stephen Crane*. Minneapolis: University of Minnesota Press, 1969.

Colvert, James B. *Stephen Crane*. San Diego: Harcourt Brace Jovanovich, 1984.

———. "Unreal War in *The Red Badge of Courage*." *War, Literature and the Arts* (1999): 35–47.

Crane, Stephen. *The Red Badge of Courage*. New York: Dover, 1990.

Dooley, Patrick K. *Stephen Crane: An Annotated Bibliography of Secondary Scholarship*. New York and Toronto: G. K. Hall: Maxwell Macmillan: Maxwell Macmillan Canada, 1992.

———. *The Pluralistic Philosophy of Stephen Crane*. Urbana: University of Illinois Press, 1993.

Davis, Linda H. *Badge of Courage: The Life of Stephen Crane.* Boston and New York: Houghton Mifflin Company, 1998.

Follett, Wilson, ed. *The Works of Stephen Crane.* 12 vols. New York: Knopf, 1925–27.

Fried, Michael. *Realism, Writing, Disfiguration: On Thomas Eakins and Stephen Crane.* Chicago: University of Chicago Press, 1987.

Ganal, Keith. "Stephen Crane's 'Maggie' and the Modern Soul." *ELH* 60, no. 3 (Fall 1993): 759–85.

Gandal, Keith. *The Virtues of the Vicious: Jacob Riis, Stephen Crane and the Spectacle of the Slum.* New York: Oxford University Press, 1997.

Golemba, Henry. "'Distant Dinners' in Crane's *Maggie:* Representing 'the Other Half,'" *Essays in Literature* 21, no. 2 (Fall 1994): 235–50.

Gullason, Thomas A. *Stephen Crane's Career: Perspectives and Evaluations.* New York: New York University Press, 1972.

———, ed. *The Complete Novels of Stephen Crane.* Garden City: Doubleday, 1967.

———, ed. *The Complete Short Stories and Sketches of Stephen Crane.* Garden City: Doubleday, 1967.

Halliburton, David. *The Color of the Sky: A Study of Stephen Crane.* Cambridge and New York: Cambridge University Press, 1989.

Heller, Arno. *Experiments with the Novel of Maturation: Henry James and Stephen Crane.* Innsbruck: Institute of Sprachwissenschaft d. University Innsbruck, 1976.

Herzberg, Max J., ed. *The Red Badge of Courage.* New York: D. Appleton and Co., 1926.

Holton, Milne. *Cylinder of Vision: The Fiction and Journalistic Writing of Stephen Crane.* Baton Rouge: Louisiana State University Press, 1972.

Horwitz, Howard. "Maggie and the Sociological Paradigm," *American Literary History* 10, no. 4 (Winter 1998): 606–38.

Johnson, Claudia D. *Understanding the* Red Badge of Courage: *A Student Casebook to Issues, Sources and Historical Documents.* Westport, Conn.: Greenwood Press, 1998.

LaRocca, Charles, J., ed. *The Red Badge of Courage.* 1st edition, historically annotated. Fleischmanns, New York: Purple Mountain Press, 1995.

Levenson, J. C. "*The Red Badge of Courage* and McTeague: Passage to Modernity." *The Cambridge Companion to American Realism and Naturalism: Howells to London*. Cambridge: Cambridge University Press (1995): 154–77.

———, ed. *Stephen Crane: Prose and Poetry*. New York Library of America, 1984.

Mitchell, Lee Clark, ed. *New Essays on the Red Badge of Courage*. Cambridge and New York: Cambridge University Press, 1986.

Monteiro, George. *Stephen Crane's Blue Badge of Courage*. Baton Rouge: Louisiana State University Press, 2000.

Myers, Robert M. "'The Subtle Battle Brotherhood': The Construction of Military Discipline in *The Red Badge of Courage*." *War, Literature and the Arts* (1999): 128–40.

Nagel, James. *Stephen Crane and Literary Impressionism*. University Park: Pennsylvania State University, 1980.

Newberry, Frederick. "*The Red Badge of Courage* and *The Scarlet Letter*." *Arizona Quarterly* 38, no. 2 (Summer 1982): 101–115.

Pizer, Donald, "Maggie and the Naturalistic Aesthetic of Length," *American Literary Realism* 28, no. 1 (Fall 1995): 58–65.

———. *The Red Badge of Courage: An Authoritative Text, Backgrounds and Sources Criticism*. New York: W. W. Norton & Company, 1994.

———, ed. *Critical Essays on Stephen Crane's* The Red Badge of Courage. Boston, Massachusetts: G. K. Hall & Co., 1990.

Robertson, Michael. *Stephen Crane: Journalism and the Making of Modern American Literature*. New York: Columbia University Press, 1997.

Solomon, Eric. *Stephen Crane: From Parody to Realism*. Cambridge: Harvard University Press, 1967.

———. *Stephen Crane in England: A Portrait of the Artist*. Columbus: Ohio State University Press, 1964.

Stallman, Robert Wooster. *Stephen Crane: A Biography*. New York: G. Braziller, 1968.

Tavernier-Courbin, Jacqueline. "Humor and Insight through Fallacy in Stephen Crane's *The Red Badge of Courage*." *War, Literature and the Arts* (1999): 147–59.

Urbas, Joseph. "The Emblematics of Invulnerability in *The Red Badge of Courage*." *QWERTY* 4 (October 1994): 255–63.

Weatherford, Richard M., ed. *Stephen Crane: The Critical Heritage.* London and Boston: Routledge and Kegan Paul, 1973.

Wertheim, Stanley. *A Stephen Crane Encyclopedia.* Westport, Conn.: Greenwood Press, 1997.

———. *Stephen Crane's* The Red Badge of Courage: *A Study of Its Sources, Reputation, Imagery and Structure.* (Ph.D. Thesis, New York University, 1963).

Wertheim, Stanley and Paul Sorrentino, eds. *The Correspondence of Stephen Crane.* 2 vols. New York: Columbia University Press, 1988.

Wolford, Chester L. *The Anger of Stephen Crane: Fiction and the Epic Tradition.* Lincoln: University of Nebraska Press, 1983.

Index of
Themes and Ideas

"BLUE HOTEL, THE," 18

"BRIDGE COMES TO YELLOW SKY, THE," 18

CRANE, STEPHEN: biography of, 10, 13–18; and Garland, 17, 56; and Stendhal, 10–11; and Tolstoy, 10–11; and Zola, 56

GEORGE'S MOTHER, 13

"HOWELLS FEARS REALISTS MUST WAIT," 39

MAGGIE: A GIRL OF THE STREETS, 18, 19–40, 70; alcoholism of Maggie's parents in, 19, 20, 22, 27–28; Billie in, 22, 26; capitalism in, 70; characters in, 25–26; critical views on, 27–40; Father in, 19, 20, 26; Hattie in, 23; Jimmie in, 19, 20–21, 22, 23, 24, 25, 29, 30, 32; and journalistic representation as Maggie's mode in, 38–40; Maggie as infantile fantasizer in, 33–34; and Maggie compared to Dreiser's Sister Carrie, 31–32; Maggie in, 19, 20, 21–24, 25, 29, 30, 31–32, 33–34, 35–36, 39; Mary (Mother) in, 19, 20, 22, 23, 24, 25–26, 27–28, 32; and metaphor and metonymy, 29–30; and naturalism, 32–34; Nellie in, 23, 24, 35, 36; and no escape from slum life, 19; observing and watching in, 30; old woman in, 19–20, 22, 26; Pete in, 19, 21–24, 26, 29, 34, 35–36; plot summary of, 19–24; and Pope's Homer, 34–36; and realism of William Hogarth's *Gin Lane,* 36–38; Miss Smith in, 26; strife marring Maggie and Jimmie in, 20–21, 22, 29–30; Tommie in, 20, 26

"MAJESTIC LIE, THE," 79

"OPEN BOAT, THE," 56

O'RUDDY, THE, 18

RED BADGE OF COURAGE, THE, 16, 18, 41–89; as affirmative and humanistic work of art, 67–69; as allegory, 80–82; and ambiguity of Henry Fleming, 63–67; and American male as athlete, 82–83; animal imagery in, 68–69; and Carlyle's *Sartor Resartus,* 52–53; characters in, 51; color sergeant's death in, 11–12, 55; competition in, 70; Jim Conklin in, 41, 43, 51, 55, 58, 70; and context and audience of 1890s, 45–46; and Crane's freedom from historical or moral perspectivism, 48–49, 61–63; critical reception of, 45, 61–62; critical views on, 10–12, 52–89; and Dante, 49, 87; death in, 49, 54; different manuscript version of, 71, 75–76; ending of, 71–72; and epic, 48–50; and epistemological uncertainty, 56–57; flag in, 12, 64; and Henry Fleming as anti-hero, 77–78; Henry Fleming in, 41, 42–45, 46–49, 51, 52, 53, 54–55, 58, 59–61, 62–67, 71–72, 75–76, 77–78, 80, 81–82, 88, 89; and Henry Fleming's development from youth into manhood, 49, 58, 63–66, 68, 71–72, 75, 77, 80; and fusion of symbolism and realism, 56, 57–59; Henry's Mother in, 46, 48, 51; and heroic idea, 49, 54, 86–87; and Homer, 41, 43, 48, 49, 80–82, 85, 87; as interior monologue, 66–67; ironic reading of Henry Fleming in manuscript version of, 75–76; irony in, 50, 58, 64, 66, 71, 72, 73, 75–78, 79, 82–83, 89; Lieutenant in, 42, 51; and literary impressionism, 47–48, 59–61, 65–66, 82–83; and machine, 47; and "martial virtue" and Bellamy's *Looking Backward: 2000–1887,* 69–70; and naturalism, 46, 54–55, 56, 69; nature in, 42–43, 46–47, 54–55, 75–76, 79–80; nihilistic element in impressionism of, 10–12; and passivity of Henry Fleming, 70; plot summary of, 41–44; publication of, 45; as quest-romance, 71–72; red badge of courage in, 12, 43, 44, 64, 71, 77; and "religion of peace" and the war archetype, 78–80; religious imagery in, 54–55, 68; Bill Smithers in, 58; and soldier's spoken language, 43, 88–89; as superlative fiction of Civil War, 84–85; symbolism in, 63–64, 72; Tattered Soldier in, 43, 51, 78, 89; and trauma in myth of Civil War, 73–74; Wilson in, 44–45, 51

"SILVER PAGEANT, THE," 37

"STORIES TOLD BY AN ARTIST," 37

THIRD VIOLET, THE, 37